the Art of
LEADERSHIP

MANAGING MONEY
IN EARLY CHILDHOOD ORGANIZATIONS

Exchange Press

7700 A Street

Lincoln, Nebraska 68510

(800) 221-2864 • ExchangePress.com

Managing Money
in Early Childhood Organizations

The Art of Leadership series replaces the popular Exchange Press textbook, *The Art of Leadership: Managing Early Childhood Organizations*. The entire series demonstrates the great complexity of an early childhood leader's job. Each volume expresses the importance of one aspect of this role. Each leader will need to prioritize all these roles based on many factors, including the skills that reside within the members of his team.

These articles were originally published in *Exchange* magazine.
Every attempt has been made to update information on authors and other contributors
to these articles. We apologize for any biographical information that is not current.
Exchange is a bimonthly management magazine for directors, owners, and teachers
of early childhood programs. For more information about *Exchange* and
other Exchange Press publications for directors and teachers, contact:

Exchange Press
7700 A Street
Lincoln, Nebraska 68510
(800) 221-2864 • ExchangePress.com

ISBN 978-0-942702-63-7

Printed by Thomson-Shore Inc. in Dexter, Michigan

© Exchange Press, 2019

Cover Design: Scott Bilstad

the *Art of*
LEADERSHIP
MANAGING MONEY
IN EARLY CHILDHOOD ORGANIZATIONS

Introduction

Chapter 1: Financial Management Principles and Practices

Chapter 2: Financial Management Strategies and Tools

Chapter 3: Raising Funds to Support Quality

Managing Money as if Your Center Depended Upon It

by Roger Neugebauer

Directors of child care centers must be as effective at managing money as they are at caring for children. This lesson, had it not been learned too late, would have saved a local nursery school. This school provided a wonderful environment for children — the staff was creative and nurturing, and the parents loved the experiences their children were having. However, the school was closed shortly after the original director left. Her replacement was an outstanding curriculum planner, but she was totally unable to come to grips with managing money. After a few minor financial crises, the school was forced to close its doors.

Unfortunately, this scenario is not rare. Many child care centers and nursery schools are plagued by faulty money management.

If child care centers were highly profitable or generously funded, the consequences of ineffective money management would not be severe. Most centers, however, operate painfully close to the red ink on a daily basis. The waste of a few dollars here and the loss of some expected income there can cause a center to delay or even cancel a pay day. If income and expenses are not carefully planned and controlled, a center can go out of business in a remarkably short period of time.

In helping centers with financial difficulties, I have noticed that a few problems tend to pop up time and again. I have described below the five most common money management pitfalls, as well as some proposed remedies.

1. The Programmed-to-Fail Budget

A director draws up a budget for which projected income equals projected expenses. However, the budget will inevitably fail because faulty assumptions were made in projecting both income and expenses.

The most common mistake here is to project income by multiplying weekly fees by the number of spaces in the center by the number of weeks the program is open. This does project a center's maximum potential income if every space is filled for every week. But this will never happen! Inevitably, a few children will leave the school in the middle of the year, and a lag of a week or more will occur before they are replaced; or a child will leave with two months remaining in the school year, and the space won't be filled; or a family will move out of town and neglect to pay their past due fees; or the welfare department will refuse to provide reimbursement for several snow days. A center that fails to account for shortfalls such as these in planning its budget will find that it never quite has enough money to pay all of its bills.

For a new center, it is difficult to predict what the shortfall in income will be. It might be risky to expect more than 60% of potential income in the first year.

For an older center, the shortfall can probably be reasonably estimated based on previous years' experiences. To calculate the maximum potential income the center could have received in the past 12 months, divide this amount into the amount of income the center actually received for the 12 months. For example, if a center had a maximum potential income of $50,000 for last year, but only received $45,000, this means it only received 90% of its potential income ($45,000 ÷ $50,000 = .90 or 90%). For the coming year, this center should set its budget no higher than 90% of its potential income.

Centers often under-project expenses by failing to include certain line items altogether. Most frequently neglected are expenses for staff training, leave time,

salary increases, fuel cost increases, and major appliance repairs. Some of these expenses (such as fuel and repairs) cannot be ignored — money must be found to pay for them. Others (such as training and salary increases) can be ignored, and frequently are, but only at the cost of severely undermining staff morale and program quality.

2. Penny-wise and Dollar-foolish Cost Cutting

A center short of funds responds by vigorously cracking down on expenditures for supplies. Napkins are cut in half, drawing is done on recycled computer paper, and free materials are scrounged everywhere.

Such a response is typical, and usually it is ineffective. Even if the average center cut its supply costs in half (which would begin to have a noticeable impact on curriculum quality), the net effect would be to only reduce the center's overall costs by about 1%.

This does not mean that centers shouldn't try to save money on supplies. Certainly all centers have an obligation to parents to keep costs as low as possible. The danger, however, is that the director and teachers will

Exhibit A Hippy Dippy Child Care — Cost Savings Analysis		
Budget Item	**Annual Budget Amount**	**Percent of Reduction to Save $1000**
Teachers' Salaries	$34,500	3
Administrative Salaries	20,000	5
Program Supplies/Equipment	3,000	33
Office Supplies/Equipment	2,000	50
Nutrition	15,500	7
Occupancy	15,000	7
Health	1,500	67
Transportation	4,000	25
Training	2,500	40
Social Services	2,000	50
Miscellaneous	1,000	100

work so hard on scrounging materials and other similar activities that they will begin to think they are doing all they can to solve their money problem. In other words, they will be distracted from effectively addressing the problem.

To put cost-cutting efforts into perspective, it is helpful to analyze the savings potential of each budget item (such as in the example in Exhibit A). First, the annual amount allocated for each line item in the budget should be listed. Then, the percent that each line item would have to be cut in order to save $1,000 per year should be calculated. To do this, divide $1,000 by the amount of each line item. For example, in Exhibit A, the line item teachers' salaries would have to be cut by 2.9% ($1,000 ÷ $34,500) to save $1,000.

A quick review of the resulting figures will identify those areas where significant cuts can be made without having a dramatic negative impact on the program. For example, the Hippy Dippy Child Care Center would have to cut the social services line item by 50%, the training line item by 40%, or the health line item by 67% to save $1,000. Obviously, cuts of this magnitude would dramatically alter these aspects of the program. On the other hand, there are four line items — teachers' salaries, administrative salaries, nutrition, and occupancy — which would be reduced by less than 7% if $1,000 were cut from them. These are clearly areas where Hippy Dippy Child Care staff should concentrate cost-savings efforts in order to have the least adverse impact on the program.

By going through this process, a program will quickly be able to identify three or four areas where attention should be focused in cutting costs. Unfortunately, it will not provide directions on how to make the actual cuts. No charts or formulas can relieve the pain from these decisions.

3. The Fruitless Fundraiser

A center pours considerable time and energy into a fundraising project, which generates only limited funds. For example, a local nursery school sponsors a fair every year. One year the school netted $725 after expenses. To earn this amount, parents and staff donated over $100 in cash and 500 hours in labor. If, instead, each parent had donated only $7, the center would have raised as much money with no effort.

Before engaging in any fundraising project, a center should perform a cost-benefit analysis. First, estimate the maximum amount of money the project could yield after expenses. Then, estimate the number of staff and volunteer hours required to carry out the project. Finally, divide the dollars by the hours. If the result is less than $10 per hour, the project is probably not worth the effort. From $10–25 per hour, it is of marginal value. Above $25 per hour, it is clearly worthwhile. Really successful fundraisers have been known to yield over $100 per hour.

4. Checkbook Balance Money Management

A center's director controls income and expenses solely by observing the checkbook balance. If the checkbook balance is high, the director freely spends money. If the balance is low, the director spends money cautiously and works hard to cut costs. If the balance is in the red, the director launches a fundraising project.

Such a casual day-to-day form of money management could have disastrous consequences for the average child care center. A center could be deeply in debt but still have a positive checkbook balance because several major purchases were made on credit to be paid 30 days later. It could be forced to raise fees in the middle of the year because no funds were set aside in the fall to cover high heating costs in the winter, or it could simply run short of money at the

	Actual Activity to Date	Projected Activity to Date	Percent of Target Achieved
Exhibit B Hippy Dippy Child Care Monthly Status Report As of June 30			
Income			
Parent Fees	$15,000	$14,500	103
Title XX	11,760	13,250	89
Food Program	5,550	5,700	97
United Way	5,250	5,250	100
Fundraising	40	400	10
Total Income	**$37,600**	**$39,100**	**96**
Expenses			
Salaries	$20,810	$20,600	101
Substitutes	1,680	1,400	120
Fringe	3,260	3,200	102
Legal	600	800	75
Training	150	300	50
Rent	2,550	2,550	100
Utilities	300	350	86
Food	5,700	5,600	102
Supplies	1,200	1,150	104
Insurance	250	250	100
Loan	900	900	100
Total Expenses	**$37,400**	**$37,100**	**101**
Balance	**+ $ 200**	**+$ 2,000**	**10**

end of every month and not know why or what to do about it.

To effectively keep a handle on a center's financial status, a director must know much more than how much money is in the checking account. She must know how much money has been expended on each budget item, how much income has been received, whether these expense and income amounts are in line with what was budgeted, and whether sufficient funds are available for upcoming major expenses.

This information can all be obtained by preparing a *monthly status report*.

The **monthly status report** can be relatively easy to prepare and interpret, yet it provides invaluable information. The report format has all of the income and expense line items from the budget listed vertically on the left hand side, followed by three columns of figures. In the first column, headed **Actual Activity to Date**, is recorded the total of all income or expenses incurred for each budget item as of the last day of the month being reviewed (the closing date).

For example, in the report in Exhibit B, $15,000 in parent fees had been received and $20,810 in staff salaries had been expended as of June 30. These figures should be readily available from the center's accounting records. (To simplify the preparation of status reports, one account or group of accounts in these records should be set up for each budget item.)

In the second column, headed **Projected Activity to Date**, is recorded the cumulative amount the center had planned in the budget to have received or expended as of the closing date. Hippy Dippy Child Care had projected receiving $14,500 in parent fees and expending $20,600 in staff salaries as of June 30. These projections are derived from the budget. The easiest way to do this is to divide each budget item by 12 to arrive at a monthly figure. This figure is then multiplied by the number of the months that have passed in the budget year. In the example, the Projected figure for rent is $2,550, or $425 per month times 6 months.

For certain budget items, projections cannot be made so easily. For centers in the north, utility expenses are seldom the same every month as heating costs soar in the winter. Similarly, parent fees and staff salaries may dip in the summer months when enrollments decline. For variable items such as these, it may be necessary to project income or expenses month by month, based on previous years' experiences.

In the third column, headed **Percent of Target Achieved**, is recorded the percent of the projected amount that the center actually received or expended for each budget item. As of June 30, Hippy Dippy Child Care had received only 89% of its projected Title XX income and had spent 101% of its projected salary expenses. The percentage figure is computed by dividing the Actual amount by the Projected amount (for example, $11,760 ÷ $13,250 = 89%).

There are a number of points to check in reviewing the monthly status report. First, of course, one should check the bottom line — the **Balance** (calculated by subtracting **Total Expenses** from **Total Income**). In the example, there is a positive

balance of $200 as of June 30. This is bad news since the projected balance was $2,000.

This means that not enough money has been set aside to cover future expenses. Once a problem is found, the next step is to trace the cause by reviewing the **Percent** column. The objective here is to find income items that are significantly below 100% of the projected amounts and expense items that are significantly above 100%. In the example, Title XX income (89%) and fundraising income (10%) are both far too low and substitute expenses (120%) are running far too high.

With this report the director has discovered that even though there is money in the checkbook, there is a serious problem developing. She also knows that to correct it she must focus her attention on the problems with Title XX, fundraising, and substitutes. In addition, she can see that small surpluses are accumulating in certain expense items (legal and audit, training, and utilities), which could be shifted over to partially offset the substitute deficit.

5. The False Sense of Security

A center's board of directors requires that every expenditure be approved by the board and that every check be signed by two designated individuals. The board has adopted these requirements in order to safeguard the center's funds.

Controls such as these may seem to be foolproof. In practice, they are often foolhardy. To be effective, the two-signature procedure requires that both individuals signing any check review background documentation to be satisfied that the expenditure is appropriate. More often than not, the second person signing the checks automatically signs them, assuming that the first person has already checked them out.

The two-signature procedure can also be inefficient. If both signers are not located in the center, much time can be wasted chasing after the second person. In cases where potential signers are unavailable, major payments or a payroll can be delayed. Some centers circumvent this problem by having one party sign a number of blank checks in advance. This, of course, undermines the safeguarding aspect of the system.

In a non-profit center, having all expenditures approved by the board can also be counterproductive. It drains valuable board time and energy away from crucial policymaking and evaluative functions. Instead of developing a sliding fee scale policy, the board debates what brand of construction paper to purchase. Just as importantly in retaining decision making of this detail, the board can undermine the staff commitment and leadership. The message conveyed to the director and teachers is that they are not trusted and that their function is simply to carry out orders from above.

The biggest danger of both of these safeguards is that they provide a false sense of security. They give the appearance of security without providing it in reality.

To provide effective security, a number of approaches can be implemented:

■ All money coming into the center should be documented with duplicate copies of pre-numbered receipts.

■ All expenditures should be made with pre-numbered checks and a file maintained with backup invoices, receipts, or explanations for each check.

■ The check writing function should be separated from the bookkeeping and checkbook balancing functions.

■ In a larger center in which responsibility for purchasing is delegated by an owner, executive director, parent agency, or board of directors, two signatures should be required on all large purchases with the limit clearly established by the delegator. (Some public and private funding organizations may, of course, require two signatures on

all checks.) In addition, two signatures should be required on all withdrawals from savings accounts.

■ Someone in a position of authority should regularly review monthly status reports to seek explanations for any expense items that are exceeding budgeted amounts or income items that are lagging behind projections.

Reference

Gross, M. J., Jr., et al. (1995). *Financial and accounting guide for not-for-profit organizations* (5th edition). New York: John Wiley and Sons, Inc.

Roger Neugebauer

Roger Neugebauer is founding publisher of *Exchange Magazine* and a co-founder of the World Forum Foundation.

the Art of
LEADERSHIP
MANAGING MONEY
IN EARLY CHILDHOOD ORGANIZATIONS

1
CHAPTER 1

Financial Management Principles and Practices

Financial Management in Early Childhood Programs

by Lori Harris

Author's Note: I edited this article just days after losing my financial management-in-ECE friend, colleague, and mentor Gwen Morgan. She ignited my passion for this topic and was a treasured supporter.

I don't have a financial management degree, nor would I be considered a financial expert by that crowd. But I have been an executive director and program child care center director for a long time and have taught courses in financial management in early childhood education for colleges in New England. That, combined with the excellent brain and teaching of Gwen Morgan, gives me expertise in financing early childhood programs. Plus, I love math. Budgets and financial management give me a chance to use math in its simplest form, which, by the way, means anyone with a calculator can do it!

As leaders in our programs, we are charged with implementing policy and monitoring budgets. In many cases we are part of developing those policies, particularly around curriculum and children, staff, and materials. At the heart of this is the budget. It turns out that your budget really is policy — there is no doubt about it. Morgan and Emmanuel start out *Managing the Dollars* (2010) with this concept and it rules our budgets — or should anyway. Let me explain. If you believe your staff should have profes-

sional development, you have to pay for it somehow; either that or the staff does. If you believe you should have lots of art products, then you have to include that in your budget. If healthy eating and producing your own food are important, you must include money in your budget to accommodate those costs.

Many of us do not have control over the budgets we are responsible for monitoring. And I am amazed at the number of owners who do not work with a budget. They "know what they have to spend and just spend it" is a phrase I hear more than you can imagine. My students in Singapore collect fees in the classrooms and, basically, principals spend petty cash to meet daily needs. Access to and control over the budget creates an opportunity to help determine what is important in our programs. At the very least, understanding how budgets work and speaking budget language provides a chance at having an influence.

Many of my students currently directing programs have reported that they were able to understand and contribute to the budget in a new way when they started to understand financial concepts. Of course, a lot of it is the sense of confidence you project when speaking out of an understanding of those concepts. You can make suggestions and back them up with how items could be funded and that makes a difference.

An important point to remember is that there is a difference between developing a budget and playing the role of accountant. An accountant looks at the history of a budget, analyzing and presenting numbers that help you see what your actual costs are. A budget is an educated guess at what you will need to run the kind of program you want to have. Your accountant can advise you about some of the costs you have had in the past and then you make decisions about where to allocate costs to realize your goals.

We start with expenses because we need to know what we have to pay for before we know how much to charge. Too often programs start with income and figure out what they can expend rather than the other way around. Once we have the expenses down, we can figure out the income side and how to meet those expenses with only parent fees or parent fees and other income of some sort.

Budget basics are simple: Money comes in and money goes out. Many people exclaim that they are "bad with numbers" or "can't do math." But it turns out that most people I have worked with CAN 'do numbers,' but they were lacking some of the tools that are a part of financial understanding and the confidence to ask questions.

Line-item budgets are the basic tool we use in our programs and many small businesses. Yes, we are a small business in many ways and yet we have a variable that does not exist in most small business ventures. Our staff costs are wildly out of sync with other budget items, taking up between 60 and 80% of our budgets. We also have the issue of revenue mainly coming from parent fees. So let's walk through a

line-item budget and what to consider as you develop yours.

The operating budget of a center is typically put together in line-item form. That means the income and expenses must be captured in an organized way. Typically, in our budgets we have two categories of expense: personnel and non-personnel. Not every budget that deals with personnel splits the budget this way, but in our work it is helpful as a way to see the comparison between staff costs and other costs.

I like detail regarding personnel in my budget, so I break down this line item into positions. In addition, some of our employees receive benefits and some may not. For example, I have a line item for director, one for each of the other roles in the office, one for lead teachers, one for teachers, and one for other staff who receive benefits. There is another line item for staff who do not receive benefits; those who are part-time, consultants, and all the people you pay for service.

Benefits include all the mandatory requirements, such as the employer share of social security and worker's compensation. It also includes optional items such as health insurance, vacation time, sick time, holidays, disability, and a host of other benefits that help you keep employees. It is important to carefully consider what you can afford; the healthier your benefits, the easier it will be to recruit staff. I know that many programs have minimal benefits as it can be costly. A healthy set of benefits will cost you somewhere between 20–30% of the salary line. You can change that percentage by charging employees a part of the cost.

A commonly under-budgeted item is substitute teachers. If you offer vacation and want to maintain ratios, you need substitutes. And people get sick. It is an expense that most of us do not include in our budgets, but we pay for them in staff morale if not in dollars.

Our non-personnel items include everything else — and I mean everything. Morgan and Emmanuel

(2010) include a very handy guide in their book. I will try to capture the essence of their suggestions here. It is useful to gather your information in categories and then decide how much to break out those categories.

Occupancy is your next biggest expense after personnel. It includes whatever you pay to be in and stay in (occupy) your building. This includes mortgage or rent, utilities, and repairs and maintenance. It also includes any insurance you carry for the building and depreciation for the building itself. A note on depreciation, since we are using a term that a lot of directors don't think about. Depreciation is the reduction in value of an asset over time. For a building, and all depreciation, you will need the help of a professional accountant to determine that cost. For example, depreciation can cause cash flow problems for some budgets, but there are ways to accommodate it annually rather than in your monthly cash flow; ask your accountant or auditor.

Supplies are a large part of our programs, but a smaller part of our budgets. Supplies include everything you need for teaching and caring for children: art supplies; materials for the classrooms; and whatever you supply for caring, including diapers, wipes, and so on. It also includes food and kitchen supplies, cleaning supplies, supplies to run the office, and first aid supplies. It also includes gloves — a huge expense in our programs.

I like to keep my consumables — things we use up quickly and have to replace — separate from the other supplies in my budget. Two items I have in that category are gloves and art supplies. You don't have to split this out; I just have that preference.

We also have furniture and equipment, and some of us have vehicles. Think about what you use in the office and classrooms, as well as in your kitchen and laundry facilities. You will also have to maintain these items and fix them, so repairs and maintenance are needed in this category.

If you maintain a vehicle, consider maintenance costs and any insurance you are required to have. My experience tells me that most programs maintain a minimum of $1,000,000 in liability insurance for each vehicle!

Professional development is also often under-budgeted. Here you include any courses, training, or conferences you would like your staff to attend. Conference attendance can include registration fees, overnight accommodations, meals, and travel or employees can pay part.

Other expenses to think about include advertising, phone, technology costs, licenses, and bank charges. These costs will vary by program; I have to pay for snow plowing whereas someone in a warmer climate doesn't have to include that item, but you have more grass mowing.

Once you have all your items documented, you have to organize them and decide what you want to group together. You want your budget to be useful, so do some combining within categories. Building repairs and maintenance can be combined with materials in one line item. All consumable materials can be listed in one line and other supplies can be listed separately in a category called 'Classroom Supplies.' Your budget doesn't have to look exactly like someone else's; it needs to reflect your particular situation in a way you understand.

Income is everything you have coming in; usually the biggest income comes from parent fees. Maybe you receive subsidy payments from organizations or the government. You may charge registration fees also. Money from the USDA food program and grants may support you. All the income you have coming in must cover your expenses.

Parent fees are a touchy subject for most of us in early childhood programs because we recognize how hard it is for families to pay for the services we provide. We don't want to overcharge parents, yet we will allow our staff to subsidize our parents with their low wages. In most cases, our families make more than the staff. There are no easy answers here and the variables are many, but we must figure out how to finance in such a way that we are no longer asking our staff to subsidize families who do not need to be subsidized.

There are several options if there is a gap between income and expense. One is to cut expenses. Generally that hit is taken by staff in the form of reductions in compensation, materials, professional development and/or benefits. Another option is to increase income by raising fees; certainly, make sure your fees are appropriate to begin with and are in line with your population.

Another is to seek outside funding, which takes time and effort from someone and most programs don't go beyond the subsidies offered through the government. And finally there are shared services between programs, giving each program additional purchasing power. This model has the potential to give programs more for its money so it's worth exploring in your community. Fees for managing services can be considerable, so this is another consideration.

Financing our programs is complicated. Understanding and incorporating the concept of 'budget is policy' will go a long way towards improvement of the fiscal life — and quality of our programs.

Reference

Morgan, G. G., & Emmanuel, B. R. (2010). *The bottom line for children's programs: What you need to know to manage the money* (5th edition). Watertown, MA: Steam Press.

Lori Harris

Lori Harris is the Executive Director for the Children's Center of the Upper Valley in Lebanon, New Hampshire. She is also the owner of the Center for Learning, Adventure and Discovery, LLC, a developing outdoor classroom and training environment. She teaches Financial Management for the Champlain College Early Childhood Graduate program and for the Connecticut Credentialing system through CT Charts a Course. She is a proud member of the new Exceptional Master Leader group. Lori taught for Wheelock College in Singapore during January and February 2016.

Budgeting for Quality and Survival in the 21st Century

by R. Ann Whitehead

A great deal has changed since I began my first child care center over 25 years ago, ranging from the dramatic increase in the cost of doing business to the level of intense competition many of us now experience. Running a child care program has always been a delicate balance between what we would ideally like to do and what we can actually afford based upon our financial resources. But, now more than ever before, it isn't enough to be committed to quality programs for children, we must be able to harness and utilize our financial resources wisely so that our programs can continue to survive even during difficult and uncertain times.

It is essential for directors and/or owners to create realistic goals that reflect the actual tuition income and the financial resources available. In order to maintain control of our finances, we must develop a well thought-out budget every year, and continuously monitor and revise it as we go. It is the only way to ensure we have the resources to not only maintain our priorities but to guarantee stability in our organizations. It can no longer be something we hope to get around to; budgeting must be one of our top priorities.

According to the experts, the three most important components of running a successful business or organization are the finances (our budgets and financial decisions), the operations (our programs), and sales or income (our enrollment). These three components are like a three-legged stool: any one of the legs breaks down and the entire thing topples over. Unfortunately, the financial component is the one we are most likely to put off, because we are the least familiar with this area. Many of us are in this field because we care about children and not necessarily because we are astute business people.

Establishing Your Priorities

I routinely meet with our directors and other administrative staff each month to define our priorities and then to plan how to pay for and implement them. Once a clear set of priorities is agreed upon, it's easier to recognize what options we have and what kinds of compromises we can make.

The quality of our programs is tied to the following variable expenses, which typically fluctuate with our gross tuition:

■ Offering competitive wages and benefits to attract and keep good teachers.

■ Providing healthy food (not just convenient snack foods) for children.

- Having well-equipped classrooms and playgrounds for a wide range of developmental activities that meet our curriculum goals.

- Maintaining our facilities so they are aesthetically pleasing as well as safe for children and staff.

- Providing training programs for our staff, including both in-house and outside workshops.

Establishing Your Tuition Rate

Establishing your tuition rate is the beginning of that special balancing act. It is essential to plan your tuition rates based on what it actually costs to run your program. This may sound obvious, but *many child care providers feel guilty about charging enough to pay for their true costs!*

If we don't share those costs with parents, we must cut other expenses, which directly affect the children and the quality of our programs. If you offer quality programs that clearly demonstrate how they benefit children, you can usually charge enough to meet the cost of the program and still remain competitive.

The Budget Process

Establishing Your Projected Monthly Enrollment and Gross Income

Your own school's history is the best indicator for anticipating the following year's enrollment. If you are beginning a new program, check with other child care center owners and/or directors in your area about their experiences. Do not use arbitrary numbers that may not reflect the reality of your particular community.

Whatever criteria you use, it is always wise to be conservative. If you've had two great years and one marginal year, you might average the three to come up with your projected monthly tuition income. Personally, I never project a great year by assuming each of my schools will have peak enrollment.

Instead, I prefer to be pleasantly surprised at the end of the year.

Using the Concept of Equivalent Children

We use the concept of *equivalent children* (EC) to project our tuition each month. Equivalent children is your average tuition rate divided by your actual or projected monthly gross tuition. For instance, if our tuition rate is $600 per month and I expect about $27,000 in monthly tuition, I divide the tuition income ($27,000) by the monthly tuition rate ($600), indicating approximately 45 equivalent children.

Budgeting Your Variable and Fixed Expenses

As I'm sure you are aware, your variable expenses are those that fluctuate, usually reflecting the changes in your gross income, such as staff wages and benefits, and materials/supplies. Fixed expenses such as lease or debt payments, utilities, and property taxes are those that remain more or less constant whether or not your enrollment goes up or down.

Variable Expenses

The variable expenses are the most important aspect of our budget, and they therefore require the most monitoring. Since many of these expenses should fluctuate with the number of children enrolled, they can be directly tied to a percentage of your gross income. Good examples are your payroll, materials/supplies, and food, which ideally reflect the number of children in your program.

Since these percentages are somewhat discretionary, they should reflect your program priorities and your personal goals. If you find that you spend everything your center has earned by the end of each month, you may never create financial stability for your organization. On the other hand, to ensure quality it is necessary to spend enough to meet the needs of the children and your curriculum goals.

Tracking Actual Costs

So, after all the discussion, how do you decide what percentages to use for these various expenses? It's always important to be realistic about your current costs and your organization's goals. Payroll costs in any program can vary widely depending upon the age groups a center serves. Infant programs have significantly higher teacher:child ratios, which result in higher payroll costs, while a school-age program may have a lower payroll than a class of three- and four-year-olds. Since our programs include broad age ranges, I prefer to use the average payroll of the entire program to determine my projected payroll costs.

Budgeting Your Fixed Expenses

After you have negotiated your loans, leases, and janitorial contracts, it's easy to forget about your fixed expenses. However, these and other fixed expenses have a significant impact on your bottom line and should be monitored periodically along with the variable expenses.

Creating the Budget

Each new year I create projections for each month for each of my schools. I use the final year-end financial statement my bookkeeper gives me as the basis for my projections. Keeping in mind all the expected changes for both our variable and fixed expenses, such as any increases in our employee benefits and, of course, workmen's compensation, I try to anticipate the income and the expenses for each month. Our tuition usually steadily increases from January through May and begins to drop in June and continues somewhat downward during the summer, so my budgets reflect these fluctuations. Your budget should also have columns for your projected expenses versus the actual amounts that were spent. Once the worksheet has been created with the proper formulas, it takes a relatively short time to put numbers into the computer at the end of each month. Of course, anytime you make significant changes in your expenses, you need to revise your projections.

Monitoring Your Actual Financial Statements

Accurate and Timely Financial Statements

In a labor-intensive field such as ours, where the income margins can be relatively low, it is essential to know what your income and expenses are each month (once a quarter is definitely not enough!). Around the tenth of the month, you should have a financial statement showing both your actual variable and fixed expenses for the prior month (have your accountant or office clerk do it or do it yourself). In addition, the statement should show the percentage of the gross income for each of the expenses.

Comparing and Tracking Your Variable Expenses

The variable expenses are the most important aspect of your budget and require the most attention. These are the expenses that can make or break a child care center. All your key people must understand the necessity of your budget and be aware when spending is way beyond your projected percentages. By comparing your actual expenses with your budget, you can decide whether you need to take steps to change a troubling trend. If your payroll was significantly higher than expected, was it due to a temporary cause, such as having the flu run through your staff, or does it reflect lower enrollment than you anticipated? If this indicates a problem with low enrollment, you may have to find creative ways to lower your payroll or create a new marketing plan. It is important to recognize that any significant deviation from your budget requires your attention. Analyzing this information is absolutely essential to controlling your costs and maintaining the stability of your organization.

Tracking Your Fixed Expenses

We often have more control over our fixed expenses than we realize. It is important to consider whether loans could be refinanced for better terms or whether to pay down extra principal if you have extra cash available. One of our schools is in a leased space, and when its enrollment plummeted, I renegotiated for lower lease payments to ensure we could continue at that site. Many of us have experienced higher insurance rates because of September 11, along with an increase in workman's compensation. It is wise to consider getting alternate bids for these items from time to time.

Monthly Income After Expenses

You should also know precisely what you have in the bank at the end of each month. Do you have enough left over to pay your quarterly income taxes and to set aside something for future expenditures? For my peace of mind, I budget both for the future as well as the present. Whenever possible, I set aside a percentage of our income after expenses for future capital improvements, such as vans, new furnaces, and unexpected contingencies. Typically, I set aside money for contingencies beginning in the fall through spring knowing that our cash flow decreases in summer months. Keeping an eye on your cash flow can also help you to create your future plans.

Comparing This Month's Actual Income and Expense With Your Budget Projections

Each month, as I plug the actual expense amounts into my projections, I can clearly see whether my budget is working. If my projections are off significantly, I will change my projections for the month or even the rest of the year. This is particularly true with the monthly gross tuition, which seems to be the most difficult for me to predict, so I expect to adjust it throughout the year.

Evaluating the Item Categories

Also, if you find that certain categories in your financial statements are confusing or don't meet your purposes, it's a good idea to change the category names or add new ones.

I found that our category called "materials/ supplies" was often much higher than my budgeted percentage. I discovered that my financial person was also including materials/supplies purchased with fundraiser money into this line item. This significantly distorted the percentages for which our directors were accountable. We created a new category called "special materials/supplies," which includes only items purchased with fundraiser money. Now I have a much more accurate picture of the directors' spending for their routine materials/supplies.

Conclusion

In spite of the fact that you will spend several hours each January creating new income and expense projections, in the long run it will save you valuable time and energy throughout the year. When financial challenges arise, you will have the information to make appropriate decisions quickly. By tracking and monitoring your expenses each month, it will be possible for you to ward off small problems before they become large, out-of-control problems.

You do not have to have an MBA to run a financially viable child care center, but it is necessary to have the tools to monitor your finances and to be able to make appropriate business decisions. Each time I visit a classroom and observe our teachers supporting happy children in a wide range of meaningful and fun activities, I am reminded how important our organization is to these children, their families, the teachers, and our communities. I come away with a renewed commitment to keeping our organization on a sound financial basis for today and for the future.

References

Caplan, S. (2000). *Streetwise finance & accounting: How to keep your books and manage your finances without an MBA, a CPA or a Ph.D.* Holbrook, MA: Adams Media Corporation.

Lonier, T. (1999). *Smart strategies for growing your business.* New York: John Wiley & Son.

Bruce, A., & Langdon, K. (2000). *Strategic thinking*. New York: Dorling Kindersley.

R. Ann Whitehead

R. Ann Whitehead is the president and founder of The Child Day Schools, LLC, consisting of five child care centers and a private elementary school in the San Francisco East Bay area. Ms. Whitehead opened her first child care center in 1976 in Lafayette and opened a second facility in San Ramon in 1983. Her most recent project has been to establish the Hidden Canyon Elementary in San Ramon, which utilizes a modified integrated curriculum approach. In order to expand into neighboring communities, Ms. Whitehead has had to carefully budget her programs and create financial strategies to maintain an expanding educational organization.

Looking at Revenue in a Different Way

Playing the Slots!

by Bob Siegel

As directors of early childhood programs we are all expected to be responsible for our center's financial performance. Even when we believe or are told that we have no fiscal responsibility, we actually do, even if it's simply in terms of keeping our customers satisfied so the center can stay full. Too often, a child care director ends up in that unenviable role of middle manager when it comes to being in charge of the budget. This means that you end up with lots of responsibility, not too much actual authority, and few resources to truly handle the job. We now have the *fiscal dilemma*.

Ah, how to go about defeating the monster of the *fiscal dilemma*? Initially, when a director first learns there are budget problems or that she needs to "meet her budget this year," her first thought is to stop spending money. Too often our initial answer to everything is to find the same items cheaper. Finding puzzles at 12% less isn't the answer, yet it's our first instinct. Note that in most centers, our classroom supply allocation runs only about 1–3% of the total budget, yet it's the first place we go.

The next place we turn is toward personnel costs, often comprising 60–90% of the budget, and clearly needing attention. But it's here that we run into the age-old question of quality vs. affordability.

Personnel expenses certainly do need attention, but let's focus this discussion on the revenue side of the budget and what we CAN DO about it. Why is it that income is the last place we turn to when encountered by financial challenges? In truth, your center's income is the place where you as a director probably have the most influence, yet we don't typically see it that way. Almost all of us "leave money on the table" every year through operating decisions that we do have control over.

Over the years I have provided management training for child care directors on fiscal performance. One of the first questions I ask is, "What is your business commodity?" and then, "Give me a verb for what we do with it." This generally perplexes a group of directors who want to answer, "We educate children." In that case, is our commodity children? No, they do not belong to us. Educating children is one of the (many) services offered in our business, but it's not our business commodity. Could it be that "we serve families"? Sounds like a dinner offering… but no. Again, the families are not our property to trade upon. In fact, each family is, in reality, the customer. Let me suggest that, financially speaking, we are in the business of *leasing slots*, which is not the generally acceptable way that we typically think about what it is we do.

Given the challenges of operating a fiscally sound child care business, I recommend we begin to change the way we think about what we do — at least in financial terms. Look up at the state license on the wall and see where it states your legal capacity, telling you how many children can be enrolled at the same time. That number, in effect, has defined the maximum number of slots you can lease at any one time. Why call it leasing? The reality is that we don't sell them. A parent makes a decision to enroll her child for a specified amount of time, which in effect means she has leased one of our slots. The more slots we can lease for the greatest number of weeks per year, the better.

Now that you've learned about the concept of leasing slots, let me introduce the most fiscally important phrase into your professional lexicon: **Potential Slot Income** (PSI).

What is it? Potential Slot Income is a way of measuring how well we achieve success in our business of leasing slots. It is also the key for looking at learning about the consequences of our program operations decisions. Here's the formula to figure out what your center's PSI is:

Determining your PSI will tell you what is the most amount of money you can take in, based on the number of slots you have. Although there are sometimes small ways of increasing that potential, you should regard this number as a hard limit. Your budget should never reflect an expectation that your slot income in a given year will be more than this calculated PSI. All of this additionally assumes a demand for your services (i.e., there are kids of all ages on your wait list). If there is not an overwhelming demand, you have other problems; however the need for proper enrollment protocols still hold true. This brings us to important concept number three: **Recommended Enrollment Protocols**.

Most commonly, centers get themselves into financial difficulties well before they open their doors. This happens in the way that we configure our groups and classrooms. I offer the following Recommended Enrollment Protocols prior to opening your center.

Set up your group sizes to be exact multiples of the adult:child ratios you want to run. Setting these maximum group sizes and ratios is one of your first business decisions and is certainly influenced,

# of slots x fee charged x unit of time fee is based on		
Some examples are:		
A.	100 slots	x $125 x 52 weeks	= PSI of $650,000
	for a typical child care for 3–5-year-olds, with weekly fees		
B.	60 slots	x $400 x 9 months	= PSI of $216,000
	for a typical part-time preschool, charging a monthly tuition		
C.	80 slots	x $21.50 x 253 days	= PSI of $435,600
	for a different center, charging a daily based fee		
	or multiple formulas when you have different rates…		
D.	8 infant slots	x $160 x 52 weeks	= $ 66,560
	24 toddler slots	x $140 x 52 weeks	= $174,720
	38 preschool slots	x $120 x 52 weeks	= $237,120
		TOTAL CENTER PSI	= $478,400

and at times is also minimally mandated by external sources (e.g. licensing regs). Ultimately though, it is management that makes the final determination as to the adult:child ratios that will be in place for the program. Some examples of this would be a *two-year-olds classroom* with a group size of 14 children, operating at a 7:1 ratio; a *toddler classroom* with a group size of 12 operating at a 4:1 ratio; or a pre-school classroom with a group size of 18 operating at a 9:1 ratio.

Overlap the age group range. For example, instead of having one classroom for 12–24 months and another room for 24–36 months, set your age range at 10–26 months and the next for 21–39 months. This allows greater flexibility to "move kids up" when you actually have room for them. Educationally, this protocol also allows movement of children when it is more developmentally appropriate rather than on their date of birth. You may also want to set up mixed-age classrooms for this purpose, for example, two preschool classrooms of children three through five years of age instead of having both a three-year-old room and a four-year-old room.

Think of your slots as containing 1.00 FTE (full-time equivalency) each. Try and avoid enrolling too many part-time children; you usually end up with slots not filled at all times during the week, and the center experiences a loss of potential slot income. When you do enroll part-time children, charge a premium of at least 10–20% for part-time enrollees (e.g. if your weekly fee is $150.00, then a three-day enrollee or a .60 FTE enrollment) will be charged $90.00 plus $10.00 premium for a fee of $100.00 (a .67 FTE revenue rate).

Hopefully it goes without saying these days, but you charge for the enrolled day, not based on attendance. The fee is paid regardless of whether the child attends or not; we still incur all costs and the slot was "leased for that day."

Once your center is open, I offer the following **Recommended Enrollment Protocols for operating the center**. When your classroom is at the first

ratio maximum (such as seven enrolled children in a classroom of 14 with a 7:1 ratio), do not enroll just one child; hold that enrollment until you can enroll several more children. This avoids having to hire another teacher for "just one kid" budget-wise. There are generally two or three main periods of the year for enrollment, with the exception of infants who enroll at all times of the year. These are beginning of the school year, start of summer, and sometimes right after the New Year's holiday. If considering enrolling that eighth or ninth toddler into this classroom, review where you are in the year and what your past patterns of enrollment have been. In this case, I would probably enroll an extra child or two in this room in early September, but not in mid-February.

When you are in a situation with people wanting your services, do not take and hold an enrollment for months in the future if you feel you could fill that slot earlier. You can offer to hold a slot if the parents pay that tuition to hold it; sometimes half-tuition is enough and more reasonable. Know your waiting list movement and find out what other centers in your community do.

Upon enrollment, collect from each family the tuition for the child's first week of child care as well as the last two weeks. This security deposit assures that you are paid for the final weeks of a child's enrollment even if he or she leaves in a hurry, by obligating the parents to inform you of the child's last two weeks of care. This process also turns out to be a great PR move, in that a family always leaves liking you because their last two weeks feel like they've been free. NOTE: It can be a hardship for some families to come up with that much cash. In that case, set up a plan for them to pay an additional $25–35 per week until the necessary reserve has been built up, usually 6–8 weeks.

Assure that children at the top of your waiting list are 'pre-processed' and have their enrollment paperwork completed. This allows you to move a child into the slot without any lag time.

Understand and compute how much potential slot income you are losing out on as a result of enrolling children at a discounted rate. A discounted rate in this case means any protocol that allows a child to be enrolled under conditions where the center receives less than the full potential income for that slot!

Although we rarely use the terminology 'discount,' the intention of our enrollment decisions may not be to discount, but the effect often is. Please note that as you read down this list of possible discounts that I am not advocating that centers never offer discounts, but rather that we do not offer more than we can afford. Historically, child care has offered the following discounts:

■ **A sibling discount**, almost always for 10% less for the older (i.e., the cheaper) child.

■ **A discount for staff member's children**, most generally falls between 20–33% discount, but I've seen it for 5% up to a 100% discount… that's free if you're actually doing the math…

…and now for the discounts that are called something else…

■ **A discount in the manner of being allowed vacation time where no fees are paid**. In some communities, it's typical practice in the marketplace for centers to offer one or two weeks off where the parents can stipulate that it's a vacation week and no fees are paid. If you do offer this vacation time, your protocol should stipulate that it be arranged for in advance. This allows the possibility of shifting staff since it often occurs during winter vacation or the end of summer when attendance is low. This becomes a discount by reducing your potential income for that slot. When you compute PSI, the formula of slot capacity X rate, then is multiplied by either 51, or even 50 instead of by 52 (weeks). This in effect gives a family over a 4% discount. A more extreme version of this is when we enroll a child for only a portion of the year, often a 9-month school year or less. What we've done in effect here is allow a child to occupy a slot for only

a 70–75% rate throughout the year where we could have filled that slot with a 100% payer.

■ **Sliding fee scales and scholarships for need** are another common practice in our industry — or at least are commonly used terms. In reality, however, these are truly only scholarships or a sliding fee scale when there is a separate pot of money, not from your operating budget, available for use to replace the lost slot income. If there are no other dollars entering your budget to make up for the lesser amount you've chosen to charge that family, then it's not a scholarship, it's just a discount. In our example, when we allow a family to come on half-tuition for two months, we have in effect voluntarily given them a $540.00 discount.

■ **Children who are enrolled on contract with an outside payer** at a lesser rate than your published and budgeted rate. The most common example is children on a subsidized program rate for families with low incomes. In many states, this (CCDBG) rate is comparably lower than centers' regular rates. When you enroll these children, you again are agreeing to a discounted rate. For example, your regular fee for preschoolers is $120.00 per week, but the state rate calls for a total of $19.00 per day or only $95.00 per week for that contracted child. This is not limited to just low-income subsidies. Other discounts for outside payers also include discounts for other organizations who fund you or for partners, discounts to attract employees of a nearby corporate employer, or even children who are wards of the state.

In addition to these discounting practices, there are other common ways that we rob ourselves of some of that potential slot income that we work so hard for. The primary example is uncollected tuition. I have a simple solution: that regular fees are paid before the child receives service. If they have not been paid, the child does not get in. Do this for two or three weeks and the word will get out. It will also be most appreciated by the remainder of your parents who make the effort to always pay on time.

Most child care organizations measure enrollment success by quoting their percent of capacity enrolled. We'll report to our supervisors "the center is enrolled at 92% capacity… we have only four open slots." While simply viewing that percentage is a decent guide to how we are doing, it's now essential to go beyond that and compare our efforts to how well it is possible to do. As a beginning, figure your PSI for the last fiscal year, then look at actual slot income. Where do you stand? How much better can you do with different enrollment protocols? Here are some guidelines to assess performance, assuming that you have demand for your services.

Measure Percentage of PSI to Actual Slot Income

Under 80%. Needs work

81 to 90%. . . . . Good

91 to 95%. .Very good

Over 95% . . . . Outstanding

Please allow me to reiterate that I am NOT recommending that you never offer appropriate or necessary discounts. Just know that some practices our industry has historically engaged in result in huge losses of potential slot income. In some cases, these are the centers that are desperately in need of increased revenue.

It might shock you to discover that your own decisions around enrollment protocols have allowed dollars to be left on the table — leaving us back where we started. Here is your opportunity to change the way you do business and have the income to address some of the issues of quality as well.

Bob Siegel

Bob Siegel is the President of his own training and consulting company, Leadership Reigns, LLC. In his career, Bob has worked as a preschool teacher, long-time child care director, graduate school teacher, children's museum director, and the National Director of Children's Services for Easter Seals, Inc. As a national expert, he often provides training and consultation in the areas of inclusion, workforce issues, and the business and fiscal aspects in the Early Care and Education field. Currently, Mr. Siegel is serving on AELL Board of Directors, as well as the Board of Directors of the World Forum Foundation. During his career, he served as the Board President for the Early Care and Education Consortium and the Illinois AEYC.

Numero Uno

"Good Management Begins with Good People"

by Dennis Vicars

I think we all agree that just keeping the lights on tomorrow and then the next day is simply not good enough — our children, families, and staff deserve so much more. A financial plan, not unlike a lesson plan, gives us a map and offers contingencies and tools to measure our progress along the way. Budgeting allows us to pull the future into the present and follow the path before us to achieve our bottom-line goals.

As we all know there are numerous ways for us to reach that bottom line, much of it based on our own personal business (and life) philosophies. I, for one, have always worked under the philosophy of win-win. I cannot win unless I am giving you what you need to win. Likewise, I believe in living from abundance not scarcity. Too often I have observed schools/centers become cheap in their attempt to reach their targets. Instead of driving their top line or revenue, they'd prefer to squeeze the middle of the Profit and Loss Statement to achieve their goals. I am by no means suggesting that line items, categories, and 'the plan' are not to be followed.

In fact, there are certain times that one must adjust even beyond the budgeted line item. The question is this: Is this your overall philosophy or situational need?

First, let's discuss the sanctity of the budget and consequently the P&L. Is it more important that 'outside maintenance' was kept to $550 last month as was budgeted or is it more important that total 'Controllables' were 11.7% of plan vs. 12% budgeted? My point is this: the purity of each line item is not as important as overall performance at the end of the month. It's great that 'outside maintenance' is on track, but maybe going over $200 for a thorough front door and window cleaning this month might bring in two new families that were impressed by your crisp look and smell. Maybe that $200 extra could be saved by buying light bulbs in bulk and amortizing the cost over the next six months (contingency planning) from your 'janitorial' line item, all of which was part of your 'Controllables' budget category. Remember, the exactness of each line item is not nearly as important as meeting the overall bottom-line objectives. This is the fun part of good management — thinking your way through the process and adjusting to unforeseen variables. The flexibility, while maintaining vigilance over your bottom line objectives, allows you the ability to take advantage of unforeseen changes or opportunities. Adjusting to variables and prioritizing based on available data is what good managing is about. A well-planned budget helps that process.

Earlier, I mentioned living in abundance as opposed to scarcity. Driving the top line is such a great use of your entire team's time! In fact, it should be priority *numero uno* when it comes to realizing your budget objectives. Anything and everything you and your team does has an impact on your budgeted top line. It's the very definition of marketing. If indeed everything you and your team do impacts your top line, why not spend the time making sure it has a positive impact? Your program quality, teacher training, building appearance, commitment to customer service, community involvement, educational philosophy, cleanliness, and even smell affect your top line. I would much rather have my entire team take this on as a priority and achieve two extra FTEs per month, than have to worry about squeezing $50 out of each line item in order to make budget. What's a better priority: having your cook spend three hours a week going to Sam's Club to save $1 on a can of corn (and possibly have a worker's comp claim) or have your cook coming in 15 minutes earlier each day to have coffee, fresh rolls, and a warm, friendly smile to greet each "anxious to get to work on time" parent at the door? Simply stated, "What is a cost and what is an investment?" and "What adds value versus what looks and feels cheap?"

At the end of the day, it's about choices based on philosophy and intent. Driving the revenue line by your entire team, while controlling costs within the big picture can be an exciting experience for your center/school. Use your budget as a tool, not as an albatross, and your center/school will prosper.

Dennis Vicars

Dennis Vicars is the President of The Arista Group, Inc. In his career, Dennis has served as a child care corporate executive, preschool company founder, and advocate on both the public and private side of early childhood education. Dennis is past President of the Child Development Policy Institute (CDPI) and a former member of California's Early Learning Advisory Committee (ELAC).

Is Your Center in Good Financial Health?

by Mary Brower and Theresa Sull

Is your center in good financial health? The financial health of a child care program is rarely included as a component of quality care for children. Finances have often been left out of the discussion because money tends to be a sensitive topic. This is unfortunate. Children can be adversely affected in several ways when their child care centers are on shaky financial ground.

In a worst-case scenario, children may suffer when a center goes out of business, resulting in the sudden loss of one or more caregivers. Families need to scramble around looking for substitute child care, which may again be temporary. A child's sense of trust, which lays the foundation for psychological health, can be eroded by inconsistent care.

Chronic financial instability, however, can also be detrimental to children enrolled in the center. Lack of adequate cash flow could cause owners or directors to hire less qualified staff, resulting in fewer educational opportunities for children. When money is a problem, facilities may not be kept as clean as possible, or equipment may not be repaired or replaced as needed to ensure children's optimal health and safety. Underpaid caregivers, or those who are waiting for a tardy check, may not give their full attention to the children. Second jobs could be sapping caregivers' energy, or stress connected to

financial worries could surface as short tempers. After juggling the finances of a child care center for 12 years, one director reported, "I felt like I was only one step ahead of the sheriff."

In our experience, centers get into financial hot water when they ignore the following six symptoms of poor financial health:

■ Payments of families' fees are past due

■ Enrollment is below capacity

■ Reporting deadlines are not met for requests for reimbursement

■ Fundraisers cost more than they earn

■ Bills are not paid on time

■ Bookkeeping uses too much of the director's time

To maintain the financial health of the center, pay attention to these warning signs! If you recognize one or more dangerous symptoms, it's time for some financial therapy. Get professional help, if necessary, to avoid the most common pitfalls of child care center financial management. We've seen that centers that repeatedly violate the following six rules tend to get into financial trouble.

Collect All Fees Required of Families in a Timely Manner

Violating this rule seems to be a center's most common financial management problem. As human service professionals, we're all tempted to do a family a favor now and then. We reason that everyone runs into cash flow problems from time to time. The truth is that late payments can become habitual, especially when there are no consequences. If a family that is behind in payment of fees suddenly removes their child from the program, the center is not likely to recover the lost revenue. Realize that allowing late payment is the same as providing a loan to families. Would you make the loan out of your own pocket? Would you charge interest?

Strategies

Establish a policy regarding what fees are due, when they are due, and the consequences for families that miss a payment due date. Follow your policy to the letter. Remember that you have a business to run and you cannot run it without income.

Don't Base the Center's Budget on Enrollment to Capacity

Your center's capacity for enrollment is based on several factors including adult:child ratios and classroom square footage required by local child care regulations. Tuition, whether from family fees or sources of subsidy, is probably your main source of revenue. Based on your budgeted income you will know how much you can spend during the year in various categories, such as personnel, equipment, and materials. A program budget that factors income based on 100% enrollment is headed for trouble because that is rarely the reality. Children age out of the program. Families change child care centers. Some communities, like those connected to a university or the military, may be fairly transient, having families that move frequently.

Strategies

Base your budget on about 95% enrollment. Keep a waiting list of interested families. Advertise your services frequently, to keep the waiting list full. Anticipate children leaving and begin to recruit early so that enrollment remains high.

Meet All Reporting Deadlines so that Payments for Subsidy or Child Care Food Program Reimbursements Arrive on Schedule

That red tape is so annoying! You feel that keeping up with paperwork takes you away from working directly with children. Remember that a mismanaged center will not remain financially viable and that if the center closes, you'll lose all your opportunities to facilitate children's development.

Strategies

Keep excellent attendance records. Be sure that each child's arrival and departure are recorded quickly and accurately. Some centers record attendance using high tech tools such as smart cards, which are swiped like a credit card and record a child's arrival and departure electronically. Use computer software that makes it easy to keep attendance records. Designate responsible persons, like family members and classroom staff, to ensure that all sign-in procedures are followed.

Raise Funds Beyond those Provided by Tuition Payments

The fact is that high-quality child care is very expensive. Few families can afford to bear the full cost of child care, even when both parents work. Child care is very labor intensive, and the truth is that child care providers often subsidize our nation's families by accepting low wages.

Strategies

Take advantage of any funding opportunities that may exist in your area. In North Carolina, for example, Smart Start is the state's funding mechanism for programs that help children under five. State funds are administered by local Partnerships for Children. Child care providers may be eligible for such diverse benefits as training or playground equipment. In most communities, parents as well as local businesses may be sources of in-kind donations or volunteers. Careful consideration should be given to all fundraising ideas to determine whether enough cash can be raised to offset the time and labor required by staff and parents.

Have Enough Money in the Bank to Pay All Your Bills on Time

To stay in business, your cash flow must be adequate to cover your fixed expenses when they become due. These expenses include staff salaries, rent or mortgage, utilities, insurance, and taxes. The costs of program and office supplies, educational equipment and materials, and groceries for children's meals and snacks are a few of the variable expense items that, along with fixed expenses, make up your accounts payable.

Strategies

Set up systems to pay all bills and meet payroll in a timely manner. Don't try to choose between paying your bills and paying your staff. All financial obligations must be met each month or the center cannot remain fiscally healthy. If you are not able to meet a payment due date, contact your creditor immediately so that you can make some arrangement for payment. Also, develop a close relationship with your bank. If you manage your center's finances responsibly, your bank may be willing to extend a line of credit that you can use if something comes up that you haven't planned for.

Designate a Competent Person to Manage the Center's Finances

Too often, responsibility for financial management falls on a director who has had plenty of training in child development, but none in business. When the director must spend many hours a week with bookkeeping, other areas of child care management such as curriculum development, family involvement or even fundraising, may be neglected. Keeping the books and making financial decisions is a huge part of child care administration. Poorly managed centers frequently get into trouble, disappointing families, children, and staff.

Strategies

Decide who will have the responsibility for financial management, and be sure that the person has adequate education and experience to do the job well. You may be lucky enough to have a board member, director, or assistant director who is willing and able to take on the job. If so, provide the technology, including up-to-date child care management software, to ensure that accurate and timely reports can be filed. Make sure that the person designated stays current with tax law, financial reporting requirements, and financial management strategies. In many cases, an accountant or a paid financial management service is the answer, but be sure that the person you hire is familiar with the uniquely challenging field of child care. Monitoring the financial health of a program is essential to assuring quality child care. Sound financial management is as much a component of quality as are appropriate adult:child ratios, adequate staff education, and safe and stimulating environments. Be aware of the symptoms of poor financial health and, when you notice any, have the right prescription to nurse your center back to health.

References and Suggested Reading

Neugebauer, R. & Neugebauer, B. (Eds.). (2007, Out of Print). *Managing money: A center director's guidebook.* Redmond, WA: Exchange Press.

Cherry, C., Harkness, B., & Kuzma, K. (2000). *Child care center management guide* (3rd edition). Torrance, CA: Fearon Teacher Aids.

Finn-Stevenson, M. (1982). *Fundraising for early childhood programs: Getting started and getting results* (revised edition). Washington, DC: National Association for the Education of Young Children.

Foster-Jorgensen, K., with Harrington, A. (1996). *Financial management for the childcare executive officer.* St. Paul, MN: Early Childhood Directors' Association.

Montanari, E. O. (1992). *101 ways to build enrollment in your early childhood program.* Phoenix, AZ: CPG Pub. Co.

Whitebook, M., & Bellm, D. (1999). *Taking on turnover: An action guide for child care center teachers and directors.* Washington, DC: Center for the Child Care Workforce.

Mary R. Brower

Mary Brower was the accounting director at Child Care Services Association in Chapel Hill, North Carolina for 11 years. She has been providing financial services to child care centers for more than 15 years.

Theresa M. Sull

Theresa Sull is a research associate at the Frank Porter Graham Child Development Center of the University of North Carolina. She currently co-directs the Quality Care for Children Initiative in the District of Columbia and facilitates the technical assistance specialist training that is a key part of that project.

To Own or to Lease?

by Kathy Ligon and Shawn Riley

The question of whether to lease or own a facility to operate your business — and the decision's impact on the business operations and future value of the business — remains the single most confusing topic among educational business owners. Rarely is this question asked when a school is in the initial planning phase, as most start-up business owners lease their facilities as a means to preserve capital. The question is much more common as a company grows, builds some capital for growth, and wants to make smart decisions regarding preservation of capital for business growth and long-term value of the business and real estate. In our opinion, there is no correct answer. Everyone should consider his or her capital needs and future business strategy.

Case Study: Martha is new to the education industry and wants to open an after-school center. She is seeking a lease for a small facility to get started conservatively and wants flexible terms that will allow her to move to another site if she has more demand for enrollment than the initial site will allow. She has personal savings for the purchase of the start-up equipment and supplies and for initial operating costs, but does not have the capital necessary to purchase a building. She finds a landlord willing to lease her a building, calculates the appropriate amount of rent based on the revenue her business can generate, and enters into a five-

year lease with two five-year options to renew. She also has the ability to assign the lease to another tenant, with landlord approval, within the lease term in the event the business grows quickly and she needs to move.

As we can see in the case of Martha, a lease gives her the ability to open a new business without having a large amount of capital and gives her the ability to move as her business grows and she needs more space. Also in Martha's case, as an inexperienced operator it was easier for her to qualify for a lease than to seek financing for a mortgage.

Case Study: Elliott owns his business and intends to expand to other sites within the next 3–5 years. By leasing his real estate, he is able to use the cash that might be invested as a down payment for real estate for the purchase of businesses or for operating cash and purchase of additional equipment and materials as he grows. He intends to sell his business in 10 years and does not want the hassle of selling real estate and is not comfortable holding the real estate long term for his successor to lease. He has secured favorable terms that set a lease amount that is equal to or less than 14% of the gross revenue that his business can generate when it is 70% occupied. With 10% increases in rent every five years during the initial term of 20 years with two five-year options to renew, Elliot can easily budget his expected facility costs for the future.

Elliott also finds a lease advantageous at this point in his growth so that more cash is available for business development. He is interested in selling his business and wants to secure long-term leases that will be attractive to a buyer of the business. Elliott understands that it is critical to understand the lease terms; based on the licensed capacity of the building and the tuition rates that can be charged in his area, there is a limit to how much rent he can pay and remain financially healthy. A good rule of thumb is to project what gross revenues a business can produce when it is 70% occupied, and plan to pay around 14% of that in rent. This amount might be slightly higher (at 15%) if the building is new and maintenance will be limited. It might also be as low as 10–12% if the building is older and will require more expensive upkeep.

Case Study: Gabrielle is opening her second child care center in a new market and also owns a real estate company. She wants to lease the new building to give her the flexibility of exiting the business in the event that the new market does not perform well, and will enter into a three-year initial lease with year-to-year options to renew. Gabrielle's real estate company frequently seeks financing, so it is important to her that she not have additional debt in the event that it damages her ability to seek loans. She also likes being able to take the full deduction of rent for tax purposes. In exchange for a shorter-term lease, she has agreed to be responsible for the HVAC (heating, ventilation, and air conditioning) system and the parking lot maintenance and repair.

In Gabrielle's case, it is important that she mitigate the risk of opening in a new market with a shorter lease. Since most landlords prefer longer leases than Gabrielle is willing to commit to, she has agreed to accept the responsibility for certain maintenance items related to the building. In a typical absolute-net lease format, the tenant is responsible for all of the costs relating to the building, including real estate

taxes, property insurance, and repairs and maintenance. When the tenant is responsible for the management and cost of these three items in addition to the rent, the lease is referred to as **triple net**.

Real Estate Ownership

Real estate investing, in general, has proven to be very profitable over time, even with recent challenges in the market. However, using a significant amount of capital for a real estate investment means that there is less money to invest in the business, which typically has a greater potential for return. In addition, real estate markets are unpredictable at best, although the United States is once again experiencing modest increases in value for owner-occupied properties. Despite these challenges, there are many advantages to real estate ownership. Now is an opportune time to consider purchasing real estate. Real estate prices in many markets have dropped, and we are starting to see a strong rebound in values in some markets. In addition, the cost of financing is at historical lows, particularly for business owners who operate the business in their own real estate.

Case Study: Contessa owns a multi-site child care business and the real estate it occupies. She enjoys the flexibility to make changes to her building without having to obtain landlord consent. This saves cash because her mortgage and related expenses on the building are less than she would spend if she leased from someone else. In addition, with each month's mortgage payment she builds equity in her property and pays down the principal balance.

Contessa enjoys the flexibility of owning real estate by being able to make decisions about its use and possible changes without gaining the approval of a landlord. In addition, she received favorable mortgage terms and is saving money by making mortgage payments instead of paying rent to a landlord. She is confident in the value of her property being equal to or greater than what she paid for it when she bought it.

Case Study: Alex owns a large Montessori school and after-school center. He initially leased the property with an option to purchase at his discretion. As his business grew and became more profitable, Alex chose to invest the excess cash into purchasing his real estate. His long-term plan is to continue to operate his single site and focus on building enrollment without sacrificing quality, selling the business at its most profitable point. He wants to sell the business to a large, financially-sound competitor that will enter into a lease with Alex as the landlord, and then use the revenue stream from the lease as a retirement asset.

In Alex's situation, real estate was a good investment for his additional cash since it was not his intention to grow his business by expanding or developing additional sites. By purchasing his real estate, he gained control over the property while he continues to operate the business and secured a long-term asset that he expects will appreciate over time. Also, Alex will enjoy a future revenue stream from rental income when he sells the business and becomes the new operator's landlord.

Case Study: Beth has operated her private school for 20 years in an area where real estate values have increased substantially, since a new hospital system was built five years ago. An analysis of her real estate indicates that it might be of greater value to her if she sells it for another use. Beth intends to investigate moving her business to another facility within the same general area to preserve her enrollment, and to seek a sale of her real estate.

Beth has operated her school in an area that has grown quickly in recent years. She works with a real estate broker that is familiar with the education industry and learns that she has a real estate asset that is more valuable if she sells it for another use (other than her educational business). This is a scenario that is not unusual for business owners who have operated their companies over long periods of time in growing markets.

The Bottom Line

When considering whether to lease or to purchase real estate, it is critical to have a complete understanding of all the current and future implications for your company and to have a general idea of where you want to end up. Since each situation is unique and each individual is impacted in a different way based on his or her particular situation and long-term strategy, it is critical to analyze every element of the situation: cash flow, tax implications, expectations for rent increases and property value appreciation, interest rates, and alternative uses for the property. You will gain the best understanding by working with a real estate broker who is familiar with the educational industry and a personal tax advisor who understands how these decisions will affect your future.

The bottom line is that the decision to lease or own real estate boils down to cash in-hand and long-term plans and is as much of a personal choice as it is a financial one. As you consider your options, remember these key questions:

■ Are your capital investments capable of producing higher rates of return when they are placed in your core business cycle or when they are placed in real estate investment?

■ Are you comfortable leasing real estate from a third party and managing that relationship in a way that is healthy for your company?

■ Are you comfortable with the idea of retaining ownership of your real estate as you exit your business in the future?

Whatever your current cash and tax situations and whatever your future plans involve, taking the time to explore all aspects of real estate leasing or owning leads to great potential rewards in the future.

Kathy Ligon and Shawn Riley

Kathy Ligon and Shawn Riley are founders of Strategic Solutions Group Advisors, a team of experienced financial experts and business and real estate brokers with over 50 years' combined industry experience. SSGA focuses exclusively on supporting clients in the education industry with their business and real estate sales and purchase needs. Kathy holds a degree in Accounting and has served in various operational and financial roles in large educational organizations before founding SSGA, and Shawn earned both his BS/BA and MBA from The Ohio State University with an emphasis in Real Estate and Finance and is a licensed real estate broker in multiple states.

To Profit or Not to Profit?

That is the Tough Question

by Roger Neugebauer

Two working mothers, Jane and Bonnie, were upset when their family child care provider decided to retire. They were frustrated with the lack of good alternatives they had for the care of their children. And in talking to their friends and community leaders, they found that this frustration was widespread. Many families in their community, some well-to-do, other struggling to get by, were in desperate need of good child care.

Jane, an elementary school teacher, and Bonnie, a middle manager in a Fortune 500 company, decided to do something about this critical community need. They agreed to quit their jobs and start a center that parents could turn to with confidence.

Once they had made this exciting decision, they were confronted with a perplexing choice — should they organize their program as a for-profit or a non-profit? They consulted a range of early childhood experts on the advantages and disadvantages of the two forms of business and here is the advice they received.

Ease of Start Up

It is nearly always easier and less expensive to set up a for-profit child care organization than a non-profit one. If an individual, or a husband and wife, are going into business as a sole proprietorship, all that is required to be in business are a few simple filings with the federal, state, and local governments. If two or more individuals are setting up a partnership to operate the child care business, the filing of partnership papers with the state government is a bit more complex and may require some support from a lawyer. If one or more individuals or organizations decide to incorporate the center, the steps in pulling together a corporate filing are more complex and can entail $1,000 or more in legal fees.

The establishment of a non-profit involves two basic steps. The first step, which is relatively easy, is the filing of articles of incorporation with the state.

The second, more involved step is to make application with the IRS for tax-exempt status. Securing 501(c)3 status from the IRS is important to a non-profit — it means that individuals or corporations can take a charitable tax deduction for donations to the organization. This process can take at least six months and can cost $2,500 or more in legal fees.

Access to Capital

A major disadvantage of non-profit status is that it is not conducive to the raising of capital. Private investments cannot be attracted since non-profits cannot spin off dividends and cannot be sold to yield returns for investors. Likewise, banks are often nervous about making loans to non-profit child care organizations, partly because they do not understand this business model, but also because they dislike putting themselves in the bad public relations position of having to foreclose on community non-profits.

In theory, for-profit child care ventures have the ability to attract capital. In reality, until a child care organization has established itself as a solid business, it is not likely to easily attract support from investors or bankers. The typical for-profit center is initially founded with funds from the founders or the founders' relatives, or with a bank loan personally guaranteed by the founders. However, once a proprietary center establishes a sound track record, it gains access to the full range of financial instruments available to finance the growth of any small business.

Access to Funding

A non-profit organization typically does enjoy greater access to funding from public and philanthropic sources. Many public and private grant programs restrict availability to non-profits or yield significant advantages to non-profits in the award process. In addition, non-profits are more likely to be recipients of charitable donations from individuals and corporations. In recent years, the funding advantages of non-profits have lessened somewhat. To begin with, the distribution of public subsidies is shifting.

In the past, state and county governments distributed most child care subsidies through large contracts to non-profit child care agencies. Today, increasing proportions of child care subsidies are distributed through some form of vouchers where parents are empowered to select their own provider. As a result, for-profit providers are benefiting along with non-profits from these funds. Today, the greatest share of federal subsidies for child care result from the forgiveness of taxes under the Child and Dependent Care Tax Credit. Parents can take advantage of a federal tax credit, on a sliding scale basis, for child care fees paid to nearly any provider. Non-profits enjoy no advantage at all in this funding stream.

While non-profits remain the primary beneficiaries of philanthropic funding, this advantage is less pronounced as well. In the past 15 years, the number of families (both fee paying and subsidized) using child care has exploded. However, child care funding by philanthropic organizations, such as foundations and United Way Agencies, has grown more incrementally. In fact, less than 1% of all funding for child care today comes from philanthropic sources (Behrman, 1996).

As a result, while in every metropolitan area there may be a few large, long established non-profit child care agencies that receive a significant share of their funding from charitable sources, most non-profit child care agencies receive little if any charitable funding. Most small and mid-size non-profits lack the skills and resources to compete effectively with larger non-profits in the grantsmanship arena.

Employers are a recent addition to the private funding picture. Seeking to gain a competitive advantage in staff recruitment and retention, increasing numbers and types of employers are investing in child care as a valuable benefit. At first, companies typically provided such benefits by setting up a non-profit child care program to run a center on or near site. As employers started to realize how complicated it was to operate a center, the recent trend has been to contract out to an existing child care agency to manage child care programs for their employees. In awarding such contracts, employers have tended to favor for-profit providers who they perceive to better understand the language and psychology of business operations.

Exposure to Taxes

By virtue of their legal status, non-profit tax-exempt organizations are able to avoid exposure to many forms of taxation. If a non-profit happens to enjoy a surplus of income over expenses at the end of a tax year, this surplus is not subject to taxation. In addition, non-profits enjoy exemption or relief from many sales, payroll, property, and licensing taxes.

Many of these tax savings truly do contribute to the bottom line, particularly as the purchases and assets of the organization grow. However, the largest form of tax relief — exemption from taxes on surpluses — may not be a significant advantage for the average non-profit.

To demonstrate this point, it is useful to examine the economics of a typical non-profit center and a typical for-profit center. Let's look at two organizations serving 80 children, each having a total income of $300,000 and ending up with a 5% surplus at the end of the year.

For the for-profit center, since it is most likely organized as a sole proprietorship or a Subchapter S corporation, the center pays no taxes on the surplus. The surplus, as can be seen in the table below, is passed on to the owner who pays federal (and often state) income taxes on her salary plus the profit.

For the non-profit center, a range of scenarios is possible. If the executive director of the center takes a relatively low salary ($30,000 in example A), the surplus escapes taxation and is returned to the organization, and the director only pays taxes on her $30,000 salary. On the other hand, if the salary of the executive director is relatively high ($45,000 in example B), the center with the same operating budget enjoys no surplus at the end of the year, and the director pays taxes on her $45,000 salary.

From these scenarios it can be argued that the advantages the average non-profit enjoys have less to do with exemption from income taxes than from the low wages it pays. If a non-profit elects to pay its employees well (whether the director or the teachers), its surplus will decline and the income taxes paid by its employees will increase.

Tax Liability Scenarios			
	For-profit	**Non-profit A**	**Non-profit B**
Center Revenues	$300,000	$300,000	$300,000
Salary of CEO	30,000	30,000	45,000
Other Expenses	255,000	255,000	255,000
Annual Surplus	15,000	15,000	0
Taxable Income	45,000	30,000	45,000

As child care organizations expand beyond typical size, the tax advantages of the non-profit do start to have an impact. On the for-profit side, as profits start to increase beyond a modest increase in the owner's salary, tax liability grows at an increasing rate. For the non-profit, as surpluses grow, increasing funds are returned to the organization free of taxation.

Access to Community Support

While tax and funding advantages are often not as profound for the average non-profit as expected, access to community support is often more significant. This advantage is most dramatic in terms of occupancy costs. The average for-profit center invests nearly three times as much in occupancy costs as does the typical non-profit (Helburn). This is a result of the fact that churches and other community organizations are much more likely to contribute free or reduced cost space to non-profit centers.

In addition, businesses are more likely to donate equipment, supplies, and labor to a non-profit center than a for-profit one. In the community, a non-profit may benefit from the impression that they are more deserving.

All this is not to say that for-profits have no chance at gaining community support. A well-respected for-profit center does have opportunities to garner community support since child care is currently viewed as a valuable service. For example, office park and residential real estate developers may provide reduced cost rent to for-profit child care providers because child care is an amenity that will make their developments more attractive.

Appeal to Volunteers

As a general rule, it is probably true that a potential volunteer will more likely elect to work in a non-profit setting. And there are a number of organized volunteer initiatives, such as the federal Americorps program and similar programs operated by religious organizations, where volunteers are placed in community non-profit programs.

However, the days of a broad base of eager volunteers are over. Whether a for-profit or a non-profit, the realistic potential pool of volunteers are parents of currently enrolled students — at least those few not working full-time or in a senior enough position that they can actually afford to take time off. Parental desire to help their children has more to do with personal motivation and time availability than with the legal status of the center.

Appeal to Teaching Candidates

In the 1970s, a wave of student and parent activists entered the early childhood workforce motivated by their vision of changing the world. Today, not only are such cause-motivated workers in short supply, but in fact the supply of teaching candidates of all types is shrinking. In this climate, factors such as pay and benefits offered, the stability and quality of the center, working conditions at the center, and the charisma of the leader are much more important factors than legal status in recruiting teachers.

Appeal to Parents

Not only is the legal status of a center not an important selection factor for parents, once parents make their choice they seldom know whether the center they selected is a for-profit or a non-profit one. Most parent surveys have found that factors such as cost, convenience, safety, and teacher warmth are the most important selection factors.

Challenge of Management

Conventional wisdom holds that for-profit entities are driven to run in a business-like manner and non-profits are less motivated to be efficient. In the real world, centers of all types operate at such tight margins that any center that is not operated with sound management skills will fail.

At the extreme ends of the legal spectrum, organizations do require divergent management skills. Large non-profit child care systems serving predominantly low-income populations are required to exercise skills in grantsmanship, multi-source fund management, public contracting, public relations, and supporting families in crisis. Large, national for-profit chains, on the other hand, must excel in real estate acquisition, multi-site management, communication, and marketing.

For the bulk of the programs in the middle of the spectrum, small and mid-sized community-based non-profits and for-profits, the skills required are almost identical. Nearly all of these typical programs derive well over 90% of their income from parent fees and must focus their attention first and foremost on guaranteeing parent satisfaction.

The area where significant differences may arise is in decision making. In a typical for-profit center, control is concentrated with a single owner or a husband and wife team. This makes for a simple, if not very rich, decision-making process. In a non-profit, ownership is maintained by the community of the non-profit as defined in the articles of incorporation. This ownership is vested in the hands of a board of directors, who are empowered to set the course for the organization. This introduces more players, and more complicated procedures, into the decision-making process, but in theory has the advantage of ensuring that interests of the community are represented in decisions.

The non-profit reality is far different. In the child care world, most boards function in an advisory, not ownership, capacity. Board members, whether parents, community members, or business leaders, do not have sufficient time to invest in thoroughly understanding all the legal, financial, educational, political, and demographic issues involved in operating the center. As a result, they by and large defer to

the director in decision making. They function more as 'boards of directeds.'

That is not to say that non-profit boards are simply a necessary nuisance. Creative directors use board positions to recruit champions and allies, such as bankers, lawyers, early childhood professors, marketing specialists, accountants, and political leaders.

Risk to Management

The non-profit structure provides limited protection to board members and the director. For example, if the center fails leaving significant unpaid bills, creditors typically cannot go after board members or the director for payment. Liability is limited to the assets of the organization. In addition, insurance coverage can be secured that provides substantial, if not complete, protection to board members acting in good faith from lawsuits arising out of the operation of the center.

On the for-profit side, risks are greater. In a sole proprietorship, if a center fails, creditors can usually go after the owner for uncollected debts. If a center is incorporated, creditors are limited to attacking the assets of the corporation. However, typically the biggest debt a for-profit center has is loans taken out to finance the start-up of the business. In many cases, banks will require the owner to guarantee such loans.

Flexibility to Change

Today, because both community based non-profit and for-profit centers are primarily customer driven, they are equally sensitive to changes in consumer demand. Non-profit organizations with diverse, talented boards of directors may be more tuned into broader changes in the community or upcoming funding opportunities, but clever for-profits also do such forecasting.

When it comes to responding to changes, for-profits, with their greater access to capital, may be able to respond more quickly to demand for new or additional services. On the other hand, with the surge of interest by public officials in the lifelong impact of the early years, effective non-profits may be able to position themselves to benefit from anticipated new public funding streams.

One way in which non-profits are inflexible is in the disposition of their assets. If a non-profit is on the verge of going out of business, it can only be taken over by another non-profit. If it goes out of business, its remaining assets can only be donated to another non-profit.

Motivation for Leaders

According to conventional wisdom, non-profit organizations are mission driven and for-profit businesses are profit driven. In the real world, motivation is not so simple.

Individuals who are driven solely by the desire for economic gain would likely give child care, with its low profit margins, a wide berth. (In recent years, of course, several child care companies have gone public, resulting in large gains for their founders. However, given the hundreds of thousands of operators who have entered the child care sector in the past decade, one's chances of hitting it big are still extremely low.)

Most child care entrepreneurs have a strong belief in the importance of early education and see their business venture as making a difference for families and children. On the other hand, they do have a strong economic incentive: if their business fails, chances are they will lose their life savings as well as funds they may have borrowed from friends and relatives. Individuals who aspire to leadership positions in the non-profit sector clearly have a desire to contribute to society. Typically as they develop their leadership skills, they also become motivated to become effec-

tive in managing the business side of their organization. However, their rewards for success are limited.

If they are successful in growing their non-profit into a successful, stable community institution, they can enjoy great satisfaction in this accomplishment. Along the way, too, they will undoubtedly receive recognition in their community and their profession. And, as the organization grows, their compensation package can grow (within limits). However, when they retire, they cannot reap any financial benefits (other than a farewell dinner and a gold watch) for their contributions.

The Bottom Line

Bonnie and Jane are faced with a difficult decision. If their goal is to provide child care in a low-income community, they clearly would pursue the non-profit route. If their plan is to build up a large chain of centers with the goal of going public, they clearly would pursue the for-profit route.

However, their goal is more middle-of-the-road. They want to set up a center for a range of working families. Their best course is not at all clear. On balance, they should probably start with the assumption that they will be opening a for-profit business as it is easier to establish and offers more flexibility in changing along the way and disposing of in the end. However, they should test this assumption by reviewing each of the factors above to see if in their particular situation the non-profit route actually offers some significant advantages.

A number of factors may dictate the non-profit path. For example, they may decide that they absolutely cannot afford to risk any of their own money or that of their families. Or, there may be some well-endowed community organizations that are willing to make significant contributions to their start-up efforts.

In any case, their decision should not be made in haste, or based on unexamined assumptions. We wish them luck.

Resources

Behrman, R. (Ed.) (1996). *Financing child care. The future of children*. Los Altos, CA: The David and Lucille Packard Foundation.

Helburn, S. (1995). *Cost, quality, and child outcomes in child care centers: Executive summary*. Denver, CO: University of Colorado.

Roger Neugebauer

Roger Neugebauer is founding publisher of *Exchange Magazine* and a co-founder of the World Forum Foundation.

Expert Contributors

Although Jane and Bonnie are fictitious characters, the advice reported is real and came from the following highly-respected leaders in the early childhood world:

Mary Ann Anthony, Director of Child Care Division, Catholic Charities, Jamaica Plain, Massachusetts

Doug Baird, CEO, Associated Day Care Services, Boston, Massachusetts

Angela Barnhart, Accounts Coordinator, YMCA of Greater Halifax/Dartmouth, Halifax, Nova Scotia

Bob Benson, former CEO, Children's World Learning Centers, Evergreen, Colorado

Roberta Bergman, Senior Vice President, The Child Care Group, Dallas, Texas

Sue Connor, Educational Consultant, Providence, Rhode Island

Cynthia Conway, Director, Westminster Child Development Center, Grand Rapids, Michigan

Margaret Leitch Copeland, Administrator, State of New Hampshire Child Development Bureau, Concord, New Hampshire

Marcia Pioppi Galazzi, Executive Director, The Family Schools, Inc., Brewster, Massachusetts

Mary Ellen Gornick, President, The CPA Group Chicago, Illinois

Gwen Hooper, Director, Arlington Children's Center, Arlington, Massachusetts

Michael Kalinowski, Associate Professor, University of New Hampshire, Durham, New Hampshire

Linda Kosinski, Director, Groton Community School, Groton, Massachusetts

Gwen Morgan, Founding Director, Center for Career Development in Early Care and Education, Wheelock College, Boston, Massachusetts

Joe Perreault, Program Specialist, Army Child Care Services, Arlington, Virginia

Edna Ranck, Director of Public Policy and Research, NACCRRA, Washington, DC

Nina Sazer-O'Donnell, Director of Community-Life Programs, Families and Work Institute, Durham, North Carolina

William Strader, Professor, Fitchburg State College, Fitchburg, Massachusetts

Roy Walker, Program Specialist, Administration for Children and Families, Boston, Massachusetts

Karen Woodford, President, Summa Associates, Inc., Tempe, Arizona

2

CHAPTER 2

Financial Management Strategies and Tools

Using Metrics to Strengthen Business Leadership

Focus on Enrollment

by Louise Stoney and Libbie Poppick

The fact that most early care and education (ECE) businesses in the United States struggle to make ends meet is not news. Nor is the fact that ECE managers feel increasingly squeezed by higher standards (which often require more dollars), competitive markets (that make it difficult to increase prices), and few opportunities for third-party funding. The bottom line is that running a successful ECE business is hard. And while many challenges are beyond the control of site directors, owners, or administrators, some can be addressed. Thinking strategically about what leaders can influence, what fiscal and programmatic decisions matter most, and what data are most likely to help a program stay on track, are key to ensuring sustainability.

This article is the first in a three-part series that will explore the concept of early care and education business metrics. Part I focuses on why metrics matter, what metrics should be tracked, and how these data can be used to support full enrollment. Part II will continue the discussion with a focus on using metrics to boost fee collection, monitor cost per child, and guide decision-making with regard to cost containment. Part III will highlight dashboards that bring all these data together in one place and discuss ways that data can help inform decision-making and public policy.

Why are Metrics Important?

Business leaders concur that metrics matter. They not only help organizations focus on what is most important and drive improvement, but they tell the story of where an organization has been, where it's going, and whether or not it is on the right track. Using metrics requires three steps: **Measuring** the data to understand effectiveness, **monitoring** that data over time to see whether the situation is improving or not, and **managing** — or taking action — based on what's learned in the measuring and monitoring.

"Measurement is the first step that leads to control and eventually to improvement. If you can't measure something, you can't understand it. If you can't understand it, you can't control it. If you can't control it, you can't improve it."

James Harrington, Management Consultant

From a business perspective, ECE managers need to know answers to such questions as:

■ What are the key measures that determine our financial health?

■ How well are we meeting them?

■ What keeps us from meeting them?

■ Are we strong enough to be around for the long term?

Without solid and easy-to-understand fiscal or administrative data, legitimate concerns can easily come across as toothless whining rather than a clear statement of the problem. Funders want to know what good services cost. Policy makers ought to know if the policies they establish are helping or hindering program sustainability. Business metrics enable program leaders to effectively communicate this information.

What Metrics Should be Used by ECE Businesses?

Effective business metrics are focused and easy to understand. A busy manager doesn't have time to read a long report or analyze complex data; she needs a few measures that can guide decisions on what matters most. And those with limited knowledge of the business side of ECE (including many funders and policy makers, as well as the general public) need measures that make common sense.

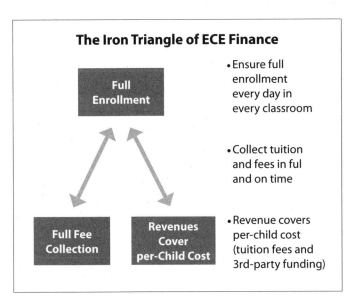

The Iron Triangle of ECE Finance

Full Enrollment
• Ensure full enrollment every day in every classroom

Full Fee Collection
• Collect tuition and fees in ful and on time

Revenues Cover per-Child Cost
• Revenue covers per-child cost (tuition fees and 3rd-party funding)

Industry leaders concur that a good place is start is with metrics that define the Iron Triangle of ECE Finance; that is, the three areas required for long-term sustainability: full enrollment, full fee collection, and revenue that covers per-child cost. This article will focus on the apex of that triangle: full enrollment. A user-friendly, recorded presentation on the Iron Triangle is available on the Opportunities Exchange website: www.opportunities-exchange.org (audio recording, PowerPoint slides).

Full enrollment is a cornerstone of ECE finance and an essential metric — regardless of whether the program relies on public funds, privately paid tuition, or both. Even when government funds a classroom of children (as is the case with Head Start or Pre-K), service providers must meet enrollment targets. The bottom line is that if children are not enrolled, the funding does not flow.

Some experts suggest that a well-run child development center can operate at 95% enrollment (Morgan & Emanuel, 2010). Reaching a benchmark this high might be possible in classrooms that receive contracts or grants, offer services free or at very low cost, or where demand is very high. In most cases, however, the industry standard of 85% enrollment is a more appropriate benchmark. And in classrooms where enrollment has been historically low, it may be necessary to drop the benchmark even lower. It is entirely possible, and in some cases appropriate, for enrollment benchmarks to vary by site and even by classroom.

ECE program managers use a variety of tools to track enrollment. Some have created 'dashboards' that enable them to monitor enrollment by classroom each week (see table on the following page). Others use an automated child management system (such as ProCare) to generate weekly reports.

Any time enrollment drops below the budgeted target, an ECE program is losing money. Thus, it is essential to set enrollment benchmarks that are informed by revenue projections, monitor enrollment on a regular basis, and be prepared

Happy Acres Child Development Center Enrollment — week of 10/26/2015				
Room	Capacity	Goal @ 85% capacity	# Enrolled	% Capacity Enrolled
Infant	10	9	9	90
Toddler	14	12	13	93
3–4 AM	16	16	15	94
3–4 PM	16	16	12	75
3s	16	12	10	63
4s	16	12	11	69
SACC	20	15	11	55
Total	108	92	81	75

underscores that the problem lies with older-age classrooms (enrollment is on target in the infant room and exceeding the target in the toddler room). The Happy Acres director knows (from cost metrics) that lower enrollment in preschool and school-age classrooms is a double problem because the additional revenue in these classrooms helps offset higher costs in the infant/toddler rooms. If efforts to fill vacant slots in these classrooms are not successful, the center will need to implement budget cuts and consider eliminating or combining some classrooms in the future.

to take corrective action if enrollment targets are consistently missed. The Happy Acres Child Care Center example reports average enrollment at 75% — significantly below the 85% target — and

One way to keep an eye on the long-term financial impact of under-enrollment is to use a tracking chart such as the one below, which looks at the financial effects of vacancies in classrooms across two centers:

Happy Kids Child Development Center — Program Enrollment and Vacancies 1/30/15								
Classroom	Ages	Licensed capacity	Staffed capacity	FTE Enrollment	FTE vacancy	% Enrolled vs. capacity	Monthly cost per vacancy	Annual projected loss/ vacancies
Crestwood Center								
Bumblebees	6 wks.–12 mos.	0	0	0	0	—	—	—
Grasshoppers	12 mos.–2 yrs.	0	0	0	0	—	—	—
Ladybugs	2–3 yrs.	0	0	0	0	—	—	—
Caterpillars	3–4 yrs.	20	20	18	2	90	$768	($18,432)
Butterflies	4–5 yrs.	20	20	20	0	100	$768	—
Afterschool	5–8 yrs.	24	24	12	12	50	$512	($73,728)
Total		**64**	**64**	**50**	**14**	**78**		**($92,160)**
Park Place Center								
Bumblebees	6 wks.–12 mos.	8	8	8	0	100	$963	$ 0
Grasshoppers	12 mos.–2 yrs.	10	10	10	0	100	$941	$ 0
Ladybugs	2–3 yrs.	12	12	12	0	100	$833	$ 0
Caterpillars 1	3–4 yrs.	20	20	20	0	100	$768	$ 0
Caterpillars 2	3–4 yrs.	20	20	20	0	100	$768	$ 0
Butterflies	4–5 yrs.	20	20	20	0	100	$768	$ 0
Afterschool	5–8 yrs.	24	24	20	4	83	$512	($24,576)
Total		**114**	**114**	**100**	**4**	**96**		**($24,576)**

These data enable a busy director to quickly understand the problem in some level of detail. Although several Happy Acres Afterschool classrooms are not pulling their weight due to consistent under-enrollment, the problem is particularly serious at the Crestwood Center. Thus, efforts to boost enrollment should focus first on this site.

Using Data to Change Practice: Focus Matters

Ensuring that all staff — including those in and out of the classroom — understand the importance of full enrollment is key. When teachers and site directors realize that keeping their classrooms fully enrolled helps generate the income needed to support improved wages or other quality supports, they are more likely to become active partners. Additionally, identifying staff to manage the entire recruitment process — from tracking vacancies to marketing and enrollment — can sharpen organizational focus on getting families on board as quickly as possible. Regular data reports can help all staff measure progress and stay on track.

"Vacancy reports by classroom help all staff understand the actual cost of not having every classroom full all the time."

Leslie Spina, Philadelphia Early Learning Alliance

Next: Using Metrics to Track Costs and Collections

This article focused on metrics to support full enrollment. Next we will look at tracking tuition collections and calculating per-child costs, and conclude with a discussion of dashboards that help busy directors view key metrics in one place. The metrics and approaches described are clearly not the only way to identify gaps and track progress. Our goal is to spur thinking among leaders in the field. We believe it is essential that industry leaders carefully explore and document ECE costs, revenues, program models, and administrative structures with an eye to gathering data that can strengthen technical assistance, training and education, as well as inform industry norms and public policy.

Resources

Mitchell, A., Brodskey, A., & Workman, S. (2015). "Provider Cost of Quality Calculator: User Guide." Washington, DC: U.S. Office of Child Care. www.ecequalitycalculator.com/Login.aspx

Morgan, G. G., & Emanuel, B. R. (2010). *The bottom line for children's programs: What you need to know to manage the money* (5th edition). Watertown, MA: Steam Press. Distributed by Exchange Press and Gryphon House.

Poppick, L., Kehoe, M., Levy, T., Price, D., & Spina L. (2015, June 2). National Shared Services Technical Conference. San Francisco. "Business Leadership: Using Metrics to Drive Quality and Sustainability" [PowerPoint slides]. Retrieved: http://opportunities-exchange.org/wp-content/uploads/Metrics-Final-with-Nurtury.pdf

Stoney, L. (2016). *Financing high-quality center-based infant-toddler care: Options and opportunities.* (In press, https://earlyeducatorcentral.acf.hhs.gov)

Stoney, L., & Mitchell, A. (2010). "The Iron Triangle: A simple formula for financial policy in ECE programs alliance for early childhood finance." www.earlychildhoodfinance.org/finance/finance-strategies

Louise Stoney

Louise Stoney is an independent consultant specializing in early care and education (ECE) finance and policy, and Co-Founder of both Opportunities Exchange and the Alliance for Early Childhood Finance. Louise has worked with state and local governments, foundations, ECE providers, industry intermediaries, research and advocacy groups in over 40 states. Public and private organizations have sought Louise's expertise to help craft new finance and policy options, as well as write issue briefs on challenging topics. She has helped model ECE program costs, revise subsidy policy and rate-setting strategies, re-visit QRIS standards and procedures, craft new approaches to contracting and voucher management, and more. Louise holds a Master's Degree in Social Work from the State University of New York at Stony Brook.

Libbie Poppick

Libbie Poppick is a partner with Opportunities Exchange, a non-profit consulting group promoting Shared Services in the early care and education sector. She brings to this work over 35 years of business and private foundation experience. In addition to her work with Opportunities Exchange, she is the former Executive Director, and currently trustee, of The Frog Rock Foundation, a private foundation serving economically disadvantaged children in New York. She is committed to helping build high-quality business and pedagogical practice, and brings to Shared Services strong analytic skills, financial acumen, and the desire to help organizations form effective partnerships. Libbie graduated from Northwestern University, and holds a Master's in Business Administration from the Harvard Business School.

Monitoring Fee Collection and Cost-per-Child

by Louise Stoney and Libbie Poppick

Effective business metrics are focused and easy to understand. The Iron Triangle of ECE Finance, which underscores the three areas required for long-term sustainability, is a helpful framework. Indeed, full-fee collection and revenue that covers per-child-cost form the base of that triangle.

Full-fee Collection

Full collection of all tuition and fees — including public and philanthropic subsidy as well as parent fees — is essential. All too often an early childhood program will have a budget that balances on paper, but the cash just doesn't come in the door. Successful ECE administrators stay on top of collections; they have clear payment policies, are firm and consistent with families, thorough and prompt with billing, and on top of the paperwork required by third-party funders.

The industry standard is to keep bad debt to less than 3% of revenues (Mitchell, Brodsky, & Workman, March 2015); however, exactly what unpaid fees are considered bad debt may vary among ECE providers. In general, the term 'bad debt' refers to the proportion of revenue that is not collected. Thus, any expected revenue that was used to establish a budget and calculate a cost-per-child that was not collected

is bad debt. Many states establish child care subsidy reimbursement rates that do not cover the full tuition and allow providers to charge a 'double co-payment' — the co-payment established by the state plus a second co-payment to cover the gap between private tuition and the state's reimbursement rate. State subsidy systems also may not pay for all of the days when a child is absent, and it may not be possible to collect payment for these days from the parent; this uncollected revenue is also bad debt. Sometimes providers have a sliding-fee scale or charge lower tuition for siblings; these losses could also be considered bad debt if the budget is based on an assumption

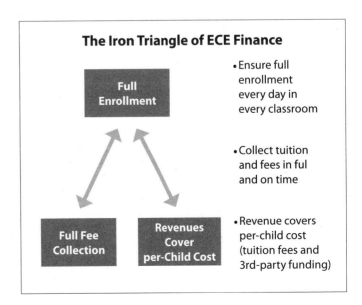

The Iron Triangle of ECE Finance

Full Enrollment

Full Fee Collection

Revenues Cover per-Child Cost

• Ensure full enrollment every day in every classroom

• Collect tuition and fees in ful and on time

• Revenue covers per-child cost (tuition fees and 3rd-party funding) that full tuition will be collected for all children. If this broader definition of bad debt is used, it may be more appropriate to establish a bad debt benchmark as high as 10% of revenues.

Regardless of the benchmark chosen, bad debt should be tracked at least monthly (many centers monitor accounts weekly) and reviewed quarterly, so that budget modifications can be made if revenues are falling short of projections. Most automated child management systems (such as ProCare) include the ability to run reports on 'account aging' that make it possible to quickly review bad debt on a regular basis.

Using Data to Change Practice: Automation Matters

Fee collection can be very time consuming unless systems are put in place to streamline and automate the process. Making electronic funds transfer the norm (that is, enabling automatic transfer of funds from a bank account, debit or credit card) is one way to strengthen fee collection. Effectively managing bad debt also requires reconciling the dollars received from government, or other third-party sources, with what was actually billed for each child, in order to make sure that errors did not occur. In many cases there is a limited amount of time to correct errors, after which funds may not be recovered.

While automated systems make the process easier, effective fee collection requires time and focus — two commodities that are often in short supply – as well as the capacity to be 'kind but firm' with families. Fee collection can be especially challenging for family child care providers, who often develop close relationships with the families they serve, making it difficult to also hold them accountable for payment. A Shared Service Alliance (or staffed Family Child Care Network) can significantly lower bad debt and boost provider revenue by centralizing responsibility for business tasks like enrollment, billing, and fee collection. This approach enables direct services staff

to focus on building a relationship with the family, and engaging in regular communication, based on supporting the child's development rather than money matters. Business tasks can be handled by another professional, whose sole focus is ensuring that fiscal transactions, and other administrative duties, are handled quickly, efficiently, and with appropriate focus on respectful customer service.

Separating business and pedagogical tasks works. One large, multi-site organization was able to reduce bad debt to less than 2% of tuition revenues after centralizing and automating its fee collection process. This central enrollment office now uses a child management system to maintain enrollment information and track parent fees. Parents are billed a week in advance and can pay by electronic bank transfer, debit card, credit card, cash, or check. Those who have not paid by the beginning of the week are alerted when they check their child in each day via the automated sign-in system; if not paid within a few days of that alert, late fees are assessed. Due to improved systems, this organization has now set a goal of keeping bad debt to only 1% of tuition revenue. Another newer and smaller Shared Service Alliance that recently replaced paper transactions with an automated child management system found that bad debt began to decline quickly, and — even more importantly — the site director significantly reduced the amount of time spent collecting and reporting finances. That freed-up time is now available to focus on pedagogical leadership and family supports.

Revenues Cover per-Child Cost

Setting tuition fees (prices) accurately involves many factors and decision points, some of which are beyond the control of an ECE program. What parents can afford to pay is based on what they earn and the local cost of living. What government, or other scholarship programs, will pay is typically based on available funds. That said, determining the actual cost-per-child, comparing this cost to the price charged, and when fees cannot cover the full cost, identifying third-party funding to fill the gap, is essential to sound fiscal management. Parent fees plus third-party payments must equal per-child cost. Otherwise the program is losing money.

The bottom line is that all three 'legs' of the Iron Triangle not only matter, but are interrelated. In tough fiscal times, when third-party funders are cutting budgets and parents are squeezed financially, ECE programs often face a difficult choice: keep fees high and risk increased vacancy rates and higher bad debt, or lower fees to boost cash flow. Unfortunately, the right answer is not simple or obvious, and it may vary from center to center based on the services offered and the families served. Thus, the more information a program director has, and the more she knows about how business metrics typically vary by time of year or ages of children or among specific classrooms or sites, the better able they are to make informed decisions and advocate for change.

The cost-per-child can, and should, be established in multiple ways. In center-based care it is helpful to know the average cost-per-child, regardless of age, as well as the cost-per-classroom and, if appropriate, per site. A different approach should be used for family child care, and will be discussed later. To calculate the cost-per-child, the following information is needed:

- Staffing by classroom or age — the number of Full Time Equivalent (FTE) paid staff in each classroom and their wages and fringe/benefit costs. Remember to build in coverage so that teachers are able to leave the classroom to participate in supervision, training, planning, child assessments, and similar activities. If children attend for more than eight hours a day, you must also include additional staff for these hours.

- Any non-teaching staff assigned to the center and their wages and fringe/benefit costs — this might include staff located in the center or, in the case of a multi-site center or Shared Services Alliance, a percentage of staff that are located in the 'hub' agency but provide administrative support to the center.

- A current budget for each center that includes all costs: classroom personnel, non-classroom personnel, and non-personnel costs.

Calculating the cost-per-child in a center requires four steps:

1. First, for each classroom or age group, add up the costs of all staff working specifically in that classroom.

2. Then decide on a method for dividing up all **other** costs, such as non-classroom staff (e.g. Director's salary) and non-personnel costs (e.g. food, utilities).

3. For each classroom add the in-classroom staff costs for those children, and all the other costs described in #2 above. This is the total cost of that classroom.

4. Divide the total cost of that classroom (the result you get in #3 above) by the average number of children enrolled in that classroom (remember to use the actual, or projected, enrollment — not the classroom capacity). This is the cost-per-child by classroom.

5. To determine the average cost-per-child in the entire center, simply divide the total cost of operating the center — including all personnel and non-personnel costs in all classrooms as well as in the administration — by the number of children enrolled.

A budget template for a non-profit or proprietary child care center, as well as tools to help calculate the cost-per-child, may be downloaded from First Children's Finance (www.firstchildrensfinance.org/businessresourcecenter/centers-2/finance/finance-tools/). Additionally, the federal Office of Child Care supported development of an online tool called the Provider Cost of Quality Calculator (https://childcareta.acf.hhs.gov/pcqc) that models the cost of providing child care services at various levels of quality and could be a helpful resource.

In Family Child Care the process is similar but simpler. Begin with a budget for the home-based business that includes all direct and indirect expenses. A family child care budget template and cash flow projection worksheet can be downloaded from the ECE Knowledge Hub or from First Children's Finance. The budget templates available from these sources will help determine the profit (or loss) from a home-based business, essentially the provider income. Using data from this budget, calculate the cost-per-child using the following steps:

1. Calculate the **current, average** per-child-cost by dividing total expenses by the number of children currently enrolled.

2. Calculate the cost-per-child **at full enrollment** by dividing total expenses by the number of children that could potentially enroll. This is typically licensed capacity or, in the event the home is participating in Head Start or Early Head Start, the total number of children allowed based on performance standards.

3. Calculate cost of care **at different ages** as follows:

   a. Calculate the cost-per-child based on the maximum number of children allowed if infant/toddlers are enrolled.

   b. Calculate the cost-per-child based on the maximum number of children allowed if NO infant/toddlers are enrolled (this typically means the provider can serve more children).

   c. The difference between (a) and (b) is the increased cost-per-child of serving infants.

4. Calculate cost of care at better wages for the provider owner by adding additional wages, as well as the cost of desired benefits like health insurance and a retirement plan, to the expense budget before calculating a cost-per-child. This could be a helpful exercise when exploring the trade-offs between full enrollment, full-fee collection, and raising rates; a combination of strategies can help stabilize revenues.

ECE program managers that maintain cost-per-child data can show that the cost of serving infants and toddlers is significantly higher than preschoolers or older children. Yet public reimbursement rates, and market prices, rarely match the actual cost differential. Data to document this concern is essential to good policy development.

However, focusing solely on the public reimbursement rate (e.g. the revenue-per-child) can be short-sighted. Experience with cost modeling suggests that other sides of the 'Iron Triangle' can sometimes make a bigger difference in a provider's bottom line. For example, increasing child care reimbursement rates will have little impact in a program that is not fully enrolled or serves a very small number of children who receive subsidy. Raising the public portion of the rate will have little impact if the parent portion (the family co-payment) is so high that providers simply cannot collect it and therefore, must maintain very high bad debt. Similarly, raising rates and lowering parent fees may not impact the bottom line if child care providers do not get paid when a child is absent or if care is not authorized for a full day or a full year. In short, ECE program managers need to understand exactly where and why they are losing money, and begin gathering the data needed to address key programs before they cripple sustainability.

Resources

Mitchell, A., Brodskey, A., & Workman, S. (2015). "Provider Cost of Quality Calculator: User Guide." Washington, DC: U.S. Office of Child Care. www.ecequalitycalculator.com/Login.aspx

Poppick, L., Kehoe, M., Levy, T., Price, D., & Spina, L. (2015, June 2). National Shared Services Technical Conference. San Francisco. "Business Leadership: Using Metrics to Drive Quality and Sustainability" [PowerPoint slides]. Retrieved: http://opportunities-exchange.org/wp-content/uploads/Metrics-Final-with-Nurtury.pdf

Stoney, L., & Mitchell, A. (2010). "The Iron Triangle: A simple formula for financial policy in ECE programs alliance for early childhood finance."
www.earlychildhoodfinance.org/finance/finance-strategies

Louise Stoney

Louise Stoney is an independent consultant specializing in early care and education (ECE) finance and policy, and Co-Founder of both Opportunities Exchange and the Alliance for Early Childhood Finance. Louise has worked with state and local governments, foundations, ECE providers, industry intermediaries, research and advocacy groups in over 40 states. Public and private organizations have sought Louise's expertise to help craft new finance and policy options, as well as write issue briefs on challenging topics. She has helped model ECE program costs, revise subsidy policy and rate-setting strategies, re-visit QRIS standards and procedures, craft new approaches to contracting and voucher management, and more. Louise holds a Master's Degree in Social Work from the State University of New York at Stony Brook.

Libbie Poppick

Libbie Poppick is a partner with Opportunities Exchange, a non-profit consulting group promoting Shared Services in the early care and education sector. She brings to this work over 35 years of business and private foundation experience. In addition to her work with Opportunities Exchange, she is the former Executive Director, and currently trustee, of The Frog Rock Foundation, a private foundation serving economically disadvantaged children in New York. She is committed to helping build high-quality business and pedagogical practice, and brings to Shared Services strong analytic skills, financial acumen, and the desire to help organizations form effective partnerships. Libbie graduated from Northwestern University, and holds a Master's in Business Administration from the Harvard Business School.

Using Metrics to Influence Policy Decisions

by Louise Stoney and Libbie Poppick

Gathering good data is key to effective management and can inform a host of decisions. However, it is easy to get buried in spreadsheets and reports and become overwhelmed by complex details. Tables, charts, or data dashboards that zone in on key metrics and provide a helpful at-a-glance picture of all relevant data are most helpful. The graphics shown display the way that two multi-site child development programs stay on top of key business metrics by using Shared Services principles to guide administration.

The first example on the following page is from Early Connections Learning Centers in Colorado Springs. This monthly monitoring report includes aggregate data from all five sites managed by Early Connections. The data is color-coded so that it is easy to see the areas that are on-target, slightly off-target but likely to attain the goal by year end, or off-track enough to warrant exploration of a course correction. The Executive Director and board review this table monthly and use it to inform management, administrative, and fiscal decisions.

The second example is from Nurtury Inc., a multi-site center- and home-based early care and education organization in Boston, Massachusetts. This table shows the business metrics tracked weekly and monthly by Nurtury, as well as the source of that data. Nurtury aims to move away from viewing data in Excel-based reports toward a simpler agency-wide 'dashboard' that allows administrators to more easily view current performance metrics by site and for the agency as a whole.

Using Metrics to Inform Policy

The child care policies established by state, local, or the federal government have a profound effect on the quality and supply of child care services — especially services available to families with low-incomes. How these policies impact the business side of ECE is key information that is often missing from the discussion. ECE programs that establish and track business metrics over time can offer invaluable information.

Good business data can help policymakers understand the impact of universal Pre-K initiatives on the supply and cost of infant care. Tracking supply at a level of detail beyond basic licensed capacity — to include the number of children who are enrolled in each classroom — can show actual use of supply and underscore trends in consumer demand. Anecdotal data suggest that many ECE programs have available slots in classrooms for three- and four-year-olds, but rarely in infant and toddler classrooms. Hard data

Early Connections Learning Centers
2015 Monitoring Report

Sustainability	April:			Year-to-Date:		
	Actual	Target	Status	Actual	Target	Status
Enrollment	83%	78%	106%	78%	78%	100%
Attendance		100%	0%		100%	0%
Total Revenue	$ 277,032	$ 266,308	104%	$1,236,659	$ 1,342,841	92%
Individuals	$ 23,255	$ 15,000	155%	$ 38,665	$ 35,000	110%
Grants	$ 2,500	$ 10,000	25%	$ 237,241	$ 298,381	80%
Events	$ 0	$ 0	100%	$ 1,500	$ 500	300%
Government (CACFP)	$ 16,781	$ 16,386	102%	$ 55,492	$ 68,355	81%
Program Fees	$ 128,087	$ 117,600	109%	$ 481,999	$ 503,802	96%
Parterships	$ 103,469	$ 107,322	96%	$ 407,177	$ 429,178	95%
Foundation	$ 0	$ 151,201	100%	$ 0	$ 151,201	100%
Net Income	($ 53,611)	$ 76,618	146%	$ 7,149	($ 18,973)	152%
Facilities						
Capital Reserve Fund				$ 4,650	$ 25,000	19%
Utilities Savings						
Depth of Quality						
NAEYC Re-Accreditation				In Proces	Yes	On Track
Child Outcomes				89%	90%	99%
Staff Recruitment & Retention						
Staff Retention	93%	70%	133%	85%	70%	121%
Terminations	0			2		
Resignations	6			11		
New Hires	2			12		

Legend:

Target is at or above budget year-to-date. No unforeseen issues are anticipated in the future.
Target is within 5% of budget year-to-date. Issues may prevent achieving the target.
Target is more than 5% off track year-to-date. Achievement of target is unlikely by year end.

that tracks these trends, and how they change over time, will be increasingly important.

ECE program managers that maintain cost-per-child data can show that the cost of infants and toddlers is significantly higher than the cost of care for preschoolers or older children. Yet public reimbursement rates, and market prices, rarely match the actual cost differential. Thus, there is market incentive to convert infant classrooms to preschool classrooms when funding from Universal Pre-K becomes more widely available. And even when

Measuring Performance: Financial and Operations		
Enrollment: central operations; program administration.	Daily full-time equivalent each week; by funding, source and program; contract utilization.	Excel. Weekly, monthly, YTD.
Enrollment efficiency: central operations; program administration.	Enrollment per provider (FCC); capacity utilization (centers).	Excel. Monthly, YTD.
Budget variance: finance.	Gross margin: by program and department.	Dynamics SL: .pdf Monthly, YTD.
Transportation: usage, reliability, cost, compliance: central operations.	Total vans, children, and children per van. Child usage by payment type and program. Incidents. Compliance.	Excel. Monthly.
Child attendance: central operations; program administration.	Review of excessive absences; EEC compliance (30 days in six months).	Excel. Monthly.
Teacher attendance: central ops; program administration.	Expected versus actual days of absences per week.	Excel. Monthly.
Provider acquisition and retention: program administration.	Providers under contract; Providers added; providers lost: by reason.	Excel. Monthly.
Teacher acquisition and retention: HR.	Retention by role and program. Staffing versus budget by role and program.	Excel/ADP. Semi-annual.

alternative funding sources are not available, ECE program managers may be forced to close infant classrooms, and shrink program size if the cost of infant care continues to drain overall center finances. Data to document this concern is essential to good policy development.

Tables that include both price and vacancy rate data can underscore how the cost of delivering ECE not only varies by age of child, but is also affected by the level of enrollment in the classroom. The following table is one example from a statewide cost analysis. While actual costs will vary based on program quality and location, cost modeling suggests that the trend underscored in this table is universal: vacant slots cost money. In tight fiscal times it doesn't make

sense to waste a single dollar. To this end, market-based child care centers that gather and analyze data on vacancy rates are in a stronger position to advocate for change and perhaps even convince policymakers to re-think how they expend public dollars.

ECE industry leaders, as well as policymakers, tend to focus most of their attention on the public reimbursement rate (e.g. the cost-per-child). However, experience with cost modeling suggests that other sides of the 'Iron Triangle' can sometimes make a bigger difference in a provider's bottom line. For example, increasing child care reimbursement rates will have little impact in a program that is not fully enrolled or serves a very small number of children

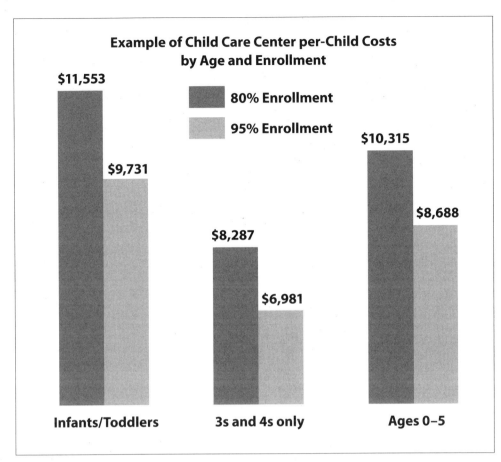

Example of Child Care Center per-Child Costs by Age and Enrollment

- 80% Enrollment
- 95% Enrollment

Infants/Toddlers: $11,553 / $9,731
3s and 4s only: $8,287 / $6,981
Ages 0–5: $10,315 / $8,688

who receive subsidy. Raising the public portion of the rate will have little impact if the parent portion (the family co-payment) is so high that a provider simply cannot collect it and, therefore, must maintain very high bad debt. Similarly, raising rates and lowering parent fees may not impact the bottom line if child care providers do not get paid when a child is absent or if care is not authorized for a full day or a full year. In short, ECE program managers need to understand exactly where and why they are losing money, and begin gathering the data needed to address key programs before they cripple sustainability.

Ways to Use Metrics to Inform Rate Policy

- Require that any entity seeking to open a new Pre-K, Head Start, or Early Head Start classroom gather data on vacant slots in all high-quality ECE programs in their target neighborhoods. First priority should be to use available funding to keep existing programs fully enrolled before adding new classrooms.

- Encourage states to use cost modeling to inform rate-setting rather than relying solely on market prices, which often do not reflect actual costs.

- Encourage higher Pre-K reimbursement rates for three- and four-year-old children in settings that also serve infants and toddlers — as a way to discourage programs from closing 0–3 classrooms to make way for (more lucrative) preschool classrooms.

- Calculate the cost of vacant slots and use this data to promote subsidy payment on the basis of enrollment, rather than attendance.

- Calculate lost revenue due to subsidy authorization for a limited number of hours a day or week, and use this data to promote authorization of full-time care.

- Explore the fiscal impact of lower subsidy co-payments or higher income eligibility where ECE programs experience high bad debt.

Next Steps

As noted earlier, this article, and Parts I and II that preceded it, suggest first steps toward thinking strategically about ECE business metrics and are intended to spur thinking among leaders in the field. Over time, industry leaders need to more carefully explore ECE costs, revenues, program models, and administrative structures with an eye to gathering data that can strengthen technical assistance, training and education, as well as inform industry norms and public policy.

Resources

Levy, T. (2015, January 2). National Shared Services Technical Conference. San Francisco. "Nurtury, Inc. Principals of Metrics and Data Management" [PowerPoint slides]. Retrieved: http://opportunities-exchange.org/wp-content/uploads/Metrics-Final-with-Nurtury.pdf

Morgan, G. G., & Emanuel, B. R. (2010). *The bottom line for children's programs: What you need to know to manage the money* (5th edition). Watertown, MA: Steam Press. Distributed by Exchange Press and Gryphon House.

Poppick, L., Kehoe, M., Levy, T., Price, D., & Spina, L. (2015, June 2). National Shared Services Technical Conference. San Francisco. "Business Leadership: Using Metrics to Drive Quality and Sustainability" [PowerPoint slides]. Retrieved: http://opportunities-exchange.org/wp-content/uploads/Metrics-Final-with-Nurtury.pdf

Stoney, L. (2016). *Financing high-quality center-based infant-toddler care: Options and opportunities.* (In press, https://earlyeducatorcentral.acf.hhs.gov)

Stoney, L., & Mitchell, A. (2010). "The Iron Triangle: A simple formula for financial policy in ECE programs alliance for early childhood finance." www.earlychildhoodfinance.org/finance/finance-strategies

Stoney, L. (2009). *Shared Services: A new business model to support scale and sustainability in early care and education.* Greenwood Village, CO: David and Laura Merage Foundation. www.earlylearningventures.org

Louise Stoney

Louise Stoney is an independent consultant specializing in early care and education (ECE) finance and policy, and Co-Founder of both Opportunities Exchange and the Alliance for Early Childhood Finance. Louise has worked with state and local governments, foundations, ECE providers, industry intermediaries, research and advocacy groups in over 40 states. Public and private organizations have sought Louise's expertise to help craft new finance and policy options, as well as write issue briefs on challenging topics. She has helped model ECE program costs, revise subsidy policy and rate-setting strategies, re-visit QRIS standards and procedures, craft new approaches to contracting and voucher management, and more. Louise holds a Master's Degree in Social Work from the State University of New York at Stony Brook.

Libbie Poppick

Libbie Poppick is a partner with Opportunities Exchange, a non-profit consulting group promoting Shared Services in the early care and education sector. She brings to this work over 35 years of business and private foundation experience. In addition to her work with Opportunities Exchange, she is the former Executive Director, and currently trustee, of The Frog Rock Foundation, a private foundation serving economically disadvantaged children in New York. She is committed to helping build high-quality business and pedagogical practice, and brings to Shared Services strong analytic skills, financial acumen, and the desire to help organizations form effective partnerships. Libbie graduated from Northwestern University, and holds a Master's in Business Administration from the Harvard Business School.

Insurance for Child Care Providers

How to Get Started

by Holly Myers

Let's face it; nobody looks forward to the insurance piece of owning or operating a business. Child care providers have a unique set of needs and exposures, and the insurance needed is no exception. It is crucial to find the right agent or broker, insurance carrier, and policies to provide the proper types of coverage for your operation and the children in your care.

Types of Insurance Representatives

An insurance agent usually contracts with one or more insurance companies and is a representative of those companies. The agent must be appointed by the insurer, which is a contractual agreement that specifies the products the agent may sell. The agreement also spells out the agent's authority to initiate a policy on the insurer's behalf. An agent with areas of expertise and coverage typically contracts with multiple insurance companies, thereby giving you insurance options to choose from.

A broker is an individual who represents the customer, but who is paid by the insurance company. Brokers are not appointed by insurers. They submit insurance applications to insurers on behalf of their clients; however, they do not have authority to bind coverage. To initiate a policy, a broker must obtain a binder from the insurer. A binder is a legal document that serves as a temporary insurance policy. A binder is replaced by a policy.

Brokers can be either wholesale or retail. If your agent or broker is unable to obtain a particular coverage you need, they may contact a wholesale broker. A wholesale broker handles specialized coverage that is not readily available to retail brokers and agents. Examples would be pollution or products liability coverage or an account with high losses. A retail broker interacts directly with the policyholder. If you purchased a policy directly from a broker, your broker is a retail broker.

Both agents and brokers have to be licensed by the state in which they operate. In order to obtain licensing, you have to go through an educational process and pass a licensing test. To retain your license, you must complete continuing education hours; the hours required vary by state. State licensing, just as in child care, reflects the minimum standards for operation.

Agents and brokers can also obtain accreditation from national accrediting bodies. Accreditation standards are established by professional associations and require higher standards than licensing standards. While accreditations are not a guarantee of excellence, they do reflect additional training. In the insurance field, an individual with a "CSRM" designation is a Certified School Risk Manager. A designation of "CIC" is a Certified Insurance Counselor. A "CRM" is a Certified Risk Manager. An "AAI" is an Accredited Adviser in Insurance. A "CPCU" is a Chartered Property and Casualty Underwriter. Accreditations indicate that education is as important to the agent as it is to you. Look for agents with one or more of these designations.

When looking for the right agent or broker for you, be sure to ask questions such as:

■ What information can you give me about your experience and expertise in selling insurance to child care providers?

■ How many insurance markets do you have for child care providers?

  • What are they?

  • Can you provide a customer referral?

■ Does the agent or broker have any accreditations?

Your goal is to find out how much the agent or broker knows about child care. If it is feasible, request that the agent meet with you, as this will ease the application process and give the agent an opportunity to tour your facility.

Types of Carriers in the Marketplace

When it comes to the insurance carrier that the agent or broker is placing your business with, find out whether the carrier is 'admitted' or 'non-admitted' in your state. An admitted carrier is under higher regulatory scrutiny and usually part of a state guarantee pool; your claim will be paid if the carrier becomes insolvent. While non-admitted carriers may be financially strong and offer broad coverage, with non-admitted carriers you do not have the same recourse, especially if the carrier becomes insolvent. An agent should disclose this information when providing a quote. In California, you can find additional

information by visiting the California Insurance Guarantee Association website: www.caiga.org.

Whether the carrier is admitted or non-admitted, find out about the insurance company's financial rating. A reliable source is A.M. Best Company rating. A.M. Best uses a two-scale process, alphabetical and roman numeral (similar to grades in school). The alphabetical rates the company based on financial stability and the roman numeral rates the company based on its assets. A company with a rating of A++XV has the strongest rating. Place your business with a carrier that has a minimum of an A rating. Note that some contracts you may enter into (lease agreements, funding, and so on) may require that you place your insurance with a carrier that has a minimum of a specific rating. Ratings can change and your agent should advise you of any significant changes. More information can be found on the A.M. Best Company website: www.ambest.com.

Some insurers sell directly to insurance buyers without using an agent or broker as an intermediary; such insurers are called direct writers. Direct writers typically focus on personal lines coverage like auto or homeowners. Some, however, do offer commercial coverage for small businesses.

You want to ask questions about the quoting insurance carrier's history and current offerings:

■ How long have they been writing child care insurance?

■ Do they have insurance policy enhancements specifically designed for child care operations?

■ Do they handle their own claims?

■ Do they have any loss control services?

Over the years, carriers have been known to pull out of the marketplace when the going gets tough. An example would be in the mid-'80s when many carriers withdrew from the child care market because of sexual abuse and molestation allegations. Insurance agents had to go to wholesale brokers in order to be able to provide coverage.

It may be tempting to go with the lowest premium, but if the company just began writing child care policies and has no track record, it could end up costing you more in the long run. It is important to remember that price isn't the only criteria when purchasing comprehensive insurance.

Tips for the Insurance Purchasing Process

Insurance is a contract with the carrier. The agent is a facilitator between you and the insurance carrier. Even the best of agents can't help you properly if you are not complete and forthcoming about your operations:

- Do you use your personal vehicle to transport children?

- Do you have employees?

- Do you use sub-contractors, including independent contractors for enhanced programs?

- Do you do overnight activities?

- Do you sponsor or host special events?

- Do your events include alcohol?

- Does your lease agreement require that you insure the building, even though you do not own it?

- Have you made any improvements to the facilities such as flooring, lighting, and so on, that you are responsible to insure?

- Do you provide drop-in, sick, or special needs care?

- Have you had any losses?

- Has your insurance been canceled or non-renewed?

Disclose everything. There is nothing worse than thinking you have lined up the proper coverage only to find out later that you are ineligible because of something that was discovered that you did not disclose.

Be sure to review the insurance requirements of all contracts before you sign them. Insurance does not cover everything and once you sign the contract, you are legally liable. I have seen many lease agreements over the years where standard insurance policies do not provide the required coverage. Do you personally, or the business, have the necessary assets to cover the contractual obligations? Covering these obligations may be accomplished through cooperation and discussion with your insurance agent, broker, risk manager, and provider.

Allow time to buy the proper coverage. It is difficult to place coverage when you get a call one hour before closing on Friday afternoon and coverage is needed for an event taking place the next day, or you are opening a new center on Monday and need insurance. If you are purchasing an existing business, you will need to secure your own insurance coverage because insurance is not transferable. In purchasing your own insurance, you have separated yourself from the prior owner's loss history and payment history. My agency often get requests from a buyer to provide the same coverage as the seller, yet the purchaser has no idea what that coverage is. An agent can't disclose information about a seller's insurance coverage without permission.

In California, the exception to this is Workers Compensation insurance (when the business purchaser retains most of the employees). The experience modification factor is calculated by the Workers Compensation Insurance Rating Bureau (WCIRB) and is based on a company's prior loss experience.

When you purchase an existing business, the experience modification factor is likely to follow you and will impact your premium positively or negatively for three years. If a company has a lower loss experience than the average company for its class of business, they receive a credit modification factor. If the loss experience is higher than the average company for its class of business, they receive a debit modification factor. The debit factor results in a surcharge to the base rates. When purchasing a business, be sure your due diligence includes the experience modification. In California, resource information can be found at www.wcirb.com.

You must establish what limits to insure for. What does your balance sheet or business plan state? An agent or carrier may help guide you; however, it is not their responsibility to determine the limits you insure for. Only you know what you have invested in the business. If you have not made any recent purchases, periodically review the cost of new equipment by checking catalogs or the Internet. Check with local contractors as to the cost to rebuild in your area. If you have replacement cost coverage, you are required to be insured for the full replacement value at the time of a loss. If you are not insured to value, you have to fill the gap from your own pocket.

Become a member of a professional association; there are national and statewide organizations. A lot of insurance carriers offer discounts to those who belong to professional associations that provide comprehensive and in-depth educational services.

Many carriers require inspections of your premises and operations. It is important to comply with the inspection, as well as any recommendations that result from the inspection. Remember, these recommendations are for the benefit of your business and the children.

Once you have purchased insurance and coverage is in place, it is just as important to maintain an open dialogue with your agent. If you are offering new programs, expanding, or incorporating, let your insurance agent know. Give as much lead time as possible as some things may not be covered under the existing insurance or the insurance required may be too expensive to purchase.

Review your insurance coverage annually to be sure you are adequately protected. Too often, child care providers add a new play structure, another location, or purchase new equipment or computers and forget to notify the agent. If a loss occurs, you will not be adequately insured.

Request that your agent periodically review your coverage to determine if it is still competitive and whether all aspects of the business are covered. In the insurance industry it is recommended that you compare rates and coverage every three to five years to be sure that coverage is still competitive. Shopping around more frequently is probably not worth it unless there have been drastic changes in the marketplace. You may not need to go elsewhere if you are dealing with an agent who specializes in child care; as mentioned before, agents have multiple insurance markets to go to and will know which carriers best fit your needs. This allows you to maintain a relationship with your agent. If you have a good relationship with your agent and someone else is knocking at your door, let your agent know. Often agents will get the carrier to adjust the price or enhance the coverage. Keep in mind, price isn't everything.

We all have busy lives and nobody wants to deal with insurance. Remember though, insurance is a key part of risk management for any business. Find the right agent, carrier, and coverage and things should go more smoothly.

Holly Myers

Holly Myers has worked in the insurance industry and specialized in child care insurance since 1981. Holly is a certified insurance counselor, certified school risk manager, and certified risk manager and has been an insurance agency owner since 2005. Holly holds a masters in governance through the California School Board Association. Holly served two consecutive elected terms on the John Swett Unified School District board, one year as president.

Accounts Receivable Management

by Kathy Ligon

Collecting payments from parents is vital to maintaining the financial health of an education business and in effectively managing cash resources. Cash management and the challenges in collecting tuition are often the last considerations of business owners as they begin their businesses, and often one of the frustrations that eventually leads to exiting the business. Careful consideration in creating healthy policies is critical when developing the business initially, and most important in the daily management of practices and processes that minimize collection issues. When done right, proper accounts receivable management allows business owners and managers the time to do what they love — care for and educate children!

Possible Payment Options

■ Mandatory Bank Draft

Schools that require bank draft for payments love the ease and reliability of this option. It has been our experience that direct withdrawal (sometimes called ACH) is most successfully implemented when a center opens because parents are often reluctant to change to this option later. The center simply pulls payments from the family's checking account each week and only has to follow up on accounts that did not have sufficient funds for payment.

■ Credit Card and Online Payments

Allowing families to pay by credit card or online payment systems is increasingly popular. Parents love the ease of swiping a credit card and enjoy the benefits of rewards with using their card for a significant expense. Owners need to carefully analyze the 'swipe fee' percentage charged by credit card merchants and study whether adding that 2 or 3% charge to the customer's bill (to offset the convenience of credit card billing) will chase customers away. That extra 2 or 3% fee may not seem like that much for each individual family, but in the aggregate, center owners may be unnecessarily losing revenues with this approach.

■ Payment by Check

Still the most popular payment option, most schools accept payments by personal or business check and increasingly utilize a check scanner to avoid trips to the bank. Owners might try to slowly migrate check-writing customers to the ACH method and emphasize that parents will not have to manually write so many checks. After all, many families are utilizing automatic 'Bill Pay' services through their bank checking accounts to handle recurring payments for utilities and cable bills. Why should child care services not be afforded similar treatment?

■ Accepting Cash

Most schools prefer to avoid accepting cash payments due to the risk associated with having cash on the premises and minimizing the risk of employee or intruder theft. Some have eliminated this option altogether. However, there are still some schools that will accept payments by whatever method a family has available and will never turn down a payment! In some demographic markets, parents simply do not have bank accounts, and cash or money order is their only option. Our recommendation is that schools phase out cash payments over a 60- or 90-day period, if possible. After cash payments are completely phased out, owners may also see a side benefit — a reduction in insurance costs, since cash will no longer be on the premises.

Effective Policies Minimize Collection Issues

More often than not, schools have effective policies in place, but are not enforcing them consistently. This creates a strain on cash flow and diverts valuable time that owners and directors would rather spend on strengthening programs and services to children and parents. Make no mistake — managing accounts receivable will always take some amount of time — the objective is to be effective and efficient with that time.

The first step in accounts receivable management is to be sure that an effective policy is articulated and provided in writing to all parents. Most schools have payment policies similar to the following:

Note the significant late fee assessed for late payment in the policy statement below. Late fees are the most effective means of encouraging prompt payment; the larger the fee, the more the encouragement! Of course, another way of stating the same thing in a more positive manner could be to state tuition rates higher and give a discount for early payment. The danger to this approach, however, is that the newly stated rates might be too high for price sensitive shoppers when compared to competitor's rates, leading to the unintended consequence of discouraging enrollment.

The second step in effective accounts receivable management is repetition, follow through, and consistency. The key is to actually do the work. This could mean setting up a regular time each week where the owner or director makes accounts receivable the number one priority. As uncomfortable as it might be to make collection phone calls, think of how uncomfortable it will be if there is not enough cash to pay the bills!

We suggest using the phone or personal contact during the morning or afternoon pick-up hours rather than sending out email collection notices or notes home to parents. Email and written notes are easy to avoid and ignore. Speaking personally with each parent or a professional, persistent phone calling program, however, are more likely to yield results. Of course, schools also have the ultimate option of dis-enrollment (or threat of dis-enrollment), which should be enough to get a parent's attention.

Here is a creative idea to consider if you want to make a positive impact on weekly collections: consider moving to a pre-paid MONTHLY fee schedule (paid in advance!). This will reduce the number of checks to process, both for you and for the family; it should improve the ratio of cash on hand vs. upcoming

---

Policy

Tuition is due no later than Tuesday by 10:00 am for the current week of service. After that time, a $25 late fee will be assessed. Students with accounts not paid in full by the end of the current week will be dis-enrolled and will not receive services the following week.

expenses, and will reduce the amount of time spent on weekly collection problems to (perhaps) monthly collection problems. Delinquent parents should still be given notice that if payment is not made during the first week of the month, then dis-enrollment is possible. Do not let a monthly payment scheme result in waiting weeks to collect overdue enrollment fees.

Consistent Application of the Policy is the Key!

One common question we hear from owners is: "I haven't been enforcing my current policy. What now?" Again, it is generally non-enforcement rather than lack of policy that leaves owners vulnerable to managing large balances and putting themselves at risk of losing income when parents leave the center. The longer an account is allowed to build, the more likely it is that you will never collect it. And at the end of the day, you are not doing families any favors by allowing their account to get to the point that it is impossible to catch up. It is our suggestion that when policies are not enforced, but ownership is now ready, willing, and able to begin better enforcement, schools should then state in writing to parents a reminder of the policy and a notice of pending strict enforcement. Aan example of a letter that could serve as notice of policy enforcement:

Following such a notice to parents, the policy must be strictly enforced to prevent falling back into the same collection issue. It is very difficult to get a system consistently enforced and very easy to fall quickly back into a collection problem.

I Have a Collection Problem with a Current Family — Now What?

Another common question that is raised by owners is: "How and when do I work with parents struggling to make tuition payments?" And "Is there ever an exception to the 'no tolerance' policy?" In my opinion, yes. The long-term customer who is having an issue and is communicating with you regularly could be considered for special arrangement. Be sure that the special arrangements are in writing and are followed through on. Be very wary of the family that sends Grandma in to pick up their child to avoid seeing you and who does not communicate with you regularly. This is not a good candidate for special allowances. It is not just the income lost that should concern owners and directors. The problem of 'free rider' children also could create an imbalance in teacher:student ratios, resulting in the addition of a

---

Dear Parents,

We appreciate the opportunity to serve your family at our center and value the time that we spend with your child. Because of the increased number of families with balances due and the amount of time spent by our management team in collecting tuition, it is necessary to begin enforcing our current accounts receivable policy so that we can spend more time in program development and less time in collections.

Our current policy as stated in your parent policies is as follows (state current policy).

Effective _____ ,
(four weeks' notice generally gives parents enough time to catch up) this policy will be enforced without exception.

Thank you for your support.

Sincerely,
Owner

teacher into a classroom, or the depletion of school supplies including food or learning supplies. Owners need to think not only about the loss of income, but also the increased expense load from non-paying families.

Now that Collections are Under Control, Can You Relax? Absolutely Not!

Collections of accounts receivable is a challenge that will remain a weekly task that must be managed constantly and consistently. Owners and directors may need to go back to step two above, and realize that collecting accounts receivable is not a destination, it is a journey. NEVER hesitate to ask parents for prompt payment. Remember, it is your stewardship to not only provide for the children entrusted in your care, but to act as a responsible manager of your center's resources, including taking responsibility for collecting and managing tuition paid by parents. This includes collecting funds in a timely fashion, controlling wasteful spending, and using available cash for strengthening children's early education.

Healthy control of accounts receivable is also an indication of the overall health of the company. If you are presenting numbers to outside stakeholders such as partners or lenders, large amounts due may have a negative impact on what you are trying to accomplish. Also, if you want to eventually present financial statements to a possible buyer for their consideration in purchasing your business or real estate, problems with parent accounts are an indication that the overall health of the business is questionable.

Creating a system for management and employing it dependably are the keys to keeping your company healthy. You should not apologize for having a consistent policy on collecting tuition payments from parents in exchange for providing a safe, respectful, and engaging atmosphere for their children. After all, you will not be doing any favors to your students or their parents if you cannot keep your doors open. Start today. Do not wait to collect what is due to you. You and your staff are working too hard to neglect this simple system!

Kathy Ligon

Kathy Ligon is founder of Strategic Solutions Group Advisors, a team of experienced financial experts and business and real estate brokers with over 50 years' combined industry experience. SSGA focuses exclusively on supporting clients in the education industry with their business and real estate sales and purchase needs. Kathy holds a degree in Accounting and has served in various operational and financial roles in large educational organizations before founding SSGA.

Fourteen Steps to Cash Flow Management

by Roger Neugebauer

As anyone who has been in the early childhood business for more than a few days knows, managing cash flow is an incredibly important skill for a center director. Even a center with an annual budget showing a healthy surplus may experience brief periods where funds in the checkbook are insufficient to pay all the bills.

To discover how successful directors manage cash flow in tight times, we surveyed members of the *Exchange Panel of 300.* Summarized below are their tips for planning ahead, suggestions on what to do in the midst of a cash flow crisis, and tempting solutions to avoid.

Prepare Today

The most important steps you can take to deal with a cash flow crisis are those you take before the crisis occurs:

■ **Always budget conservatively.** A common mistake of rookie directors is to develop an annual budget based on full enrollment. Even the very best centers find it impossible to maintain enrollment at 100% as there are inevitable lags between one family leaving and another enrolling. More often centers operate at between 80% and 85% capacity. To avoid creating unnecessary cash flow

surprises, make sure that you budget income with considerable conservatism and expenses with considerable pessimism. Any surprises you experience in this mode should be pleasant ones.

■ **Build credibility with your creditors.** One of the simplest, yet most effective cash flow management steps you can take is to pay your bills on time. If you build high credibility with your creditors when times are good, you are more likely to win their support when times are not so good.

■ **Establish a line of credit.** If you are in the midst of a financial crisis, no bank is likely to rush to your rescue. Remember that a bank's practice is loaning money to people who don't need it. So the best time to arrange for a line of credit you may need to get you through a difficult patch is when your center is doing well. Go to the bank when your center's financials are strong and arrange a line of credit sufficient to carry you through two or three difficult months. Then pretend you don't have it, so you don't get complacent in your money management.

■ **Set up a rainy day fund.** An alternative, or maybe a supplement, to a line of credit is a reserve fund that you establish when the center has a surplus. When you have money in the bank, it's awfully tempting to go out and buy that new playground structure or to finally repaint the center. However, before you make these decisions, you should seriously consider salting some of these funds away into a fund to provide some cushion during hard times.

■ **Develop the habit of analyzing cash flow.** Every director should develop the discipline of analyzing cash flow year round, not just when times are tight. For at least 12 months ahead, project when income and expenses will occur. This will enable you to foresee times when expenses will exceed income, and to start taking action in advance. Some directors do these projections on a monthly basis, whereas others do them week by week (which is most important during periods of crisis). Again, as with budgeting, you should be pretty conservative in making these projections. For example, don't assume that all parents will pay their fees on time, and never assume a public agency will process invoices on time.

Work Hard to Survive

Once a cash flow crisis has set in, it's time to change tactics:

■ **Maintain confidence in your program.** Even though you as director may be under tremendous stress, you can't afford to spread your anxiety to teachers and parents. If parents think that your program is in trouble, they may start looking for other options, which will only exacerbate your problems. Likewise, if staff are worried about the survival of the center, they too may start jumping ship, or at least lose some of their motivation.

This doesn't mean, of course, that you should pretend that everything is rosy. When times are tight, staff and parents will inevitably pick up on the signs of stress. If they sense that times are a bit tight and you are acting like nothing is wrong, rumors may start to build out of proportion to reality. Rather, you should let parents and staff know that the center is experiencing a 'cash flow

crisis' while expressing confidence that this is only a temporary condition. Be honest, but confident.

■ **Manage cash flowing in.** The bottom line is that there are really only two surefire ways to survive a cash flow crisis — speeding up the flow of cash coming in, and slowing down the flow of cash going out. In the first instance, the most important way to speed the inflow of cash is to be vigilant about fee collections — making sure that invoices are processed on a timely basis, rewarding parents for paying fees early, penalizing parents for paying fees late (as long as you don't ignore usury laws, of course), and paying close attention to parents who are starting to get behind in their fees. Other less likely solutions are to move up in time scheduled fundraisers or special money making projects.

■ **Manage cash flowing out.** This is where your good bill paying behavior will pay off. If you have established a dependable payment history with vendors, they will be likely to work with you and stretch their payment terms a few weeks when you are in trouble. However, vendors don't like surprises. You will get more cooperation from a vendor you owe money to if you come to them before the payment is due and ask for some extra time, than if you wait for them to call you after the payment is overdue.

In addition, you should look for major purchases you can defer in order to improve cash flow. For example, if you are planning to purchase a new computer for your office in February, but through doing careful cash flow analysis see that the month of March is going to be a tight one, put off this purchase until May, thereby lessening the hill you need to climb in March.

■ **Carefully monitor staff schedules.** Since anywhere from 70% to 80% of a center's expenditures go for staff salaries, attention to this line item is paramount. You are trying to balance three factors — you want to maintain the quality of your services, you want to avoid over-expenditures on staffing, and you want to maintain staff morale. If you cut staff hours across the board, you will impact quality. If you have staff coming and going on an hourly basis based on daily fluctuations in attendance, you may damage staff morale. Yet, if you do nothing, you may not be able to pay your bills.

Your best bet is to explain the challenge to staff and work with them to develop as lean a schedule as possible based on attendance patterns. If you end up having a few staff members who are paying a higher price for this — working split shifts or changing their hours from week to week — make sure you show your recognition of their sacrifices and try to assure them that this is a short-term situation.

■ **Focus on solutions with a future.** During major cash flow crises, there is a temptation to reach out for quick one-shot solutions — organizing a fundraiser, seeking grants, seeking donations from current and former parents. These solutions will demand a lot of energy and time to pull off, with no guarantee of success. Rather than investing your resources into such one-shot solutions, you should consider new ventures that can fit into the long-range plans of the organization. For example, it may be a better use of everyone's time to launch a new afterschool component than to organize a pancake breakfast; to create a new one-Friday-a-month 'parents' night out' service, than to hold a center-wide yard sale.

Avoid Common Mistakes

Panel of 300 members shared some cash flow management mistakes as well. Here are a few paths not to follow:

■ **Don't delay taking action.** When an organization starts sliding into a rough patch, it's always tempting to deny what is happening and hope the crisis will pass. However, the longer a director delays in taking action, the steeper the hill will be to climb. If a director foresees a cash flow shortage looming a month away, this provides four weeks of income and expenses that can be manipulated to ease the crisis. If you wait until the crisis is upon you, your options are significantly reduced.

■ **Don't defer payroll.** Given that staff salaries constitute the bulk of your expenditures, it's tempting to take the easy way out when funds are short and to delay a payroll for a week or two. However, the risks to destroying staff morale are too great. Having a payroll delayed sends a chilling message to staff that should be avoided at all costs. Delay payroll only as a last resort.

■ **Don't defer payroll taxes.** An even more dangerous temptation is to get into the habit of delaying the deposit of payroll taxes. Too many centers have ended up paying severe tax penalties when they got caught playing this game.

■ **Don't borrow from your future.** Another temptation to avoid is to dip into funds that are designated for future activities. For example, if you collect advances from families for your summer camp, it may be tempting to use these advances to cover a cash flow gap. The problem is that come summer, the camp you won't have these funds to cover your expenses. If you do find it necessary to dip into funds for future events, make sure that your cash flow recovery plan includes provisions for replenishing these funds.

■ **Don't delude yourself.** Part of your analysis of a cash flow crisis is to decide if it truly is a 'temporary cash flow crisis' or something more serious. When a center seems to go from one cash flow crisis to another, this may be an indication that there is a fundamental problem with the financial structure of the center. Possibly your fee is simply set too low, maybe your enrollment is steadily declining, maybe your expenses are out of control. So while you are struggling through a difficult cash flow period, take a step back and analyze whether this is a temporary challenge or a more basic financial issue.

Panel of 300 Contributors

The following *Panel of 300* members contributed to this article:

Carolyn Barnes
Gateway Christian Preschool, Pensacola, Florida

Mary Lou Beaver
Dover Children's Centers, Dover, New Hampshire

Judy Chosy
Smoky Row Children's Centers, Powell, Ohio

Kathy Cronemiller
Child Care Inc., Midwest City, Oklahoma

Marie Darstein
The Sunshine House, Rock Hill, South Carolina

Betty DePina
Mountain Area Child and Family
Asheville, North Carolina

Marsha Enquist
Chicago, Illinois

Melissa Hoover
Seven Bends Student Centers, Woodstock, Virginia

Sarah Horn
Allegheny Child Care Academy, Pittsburgh, Pennsylvania

Amy Huppe
Wee Play School, Manchester, New Hampshire

Dr. Raina Jain
Witty Kids, Mumbai, India

Barbara Lynn
Community Preschool, Jacksonville, Florida

Suzanne Martin
Kids Life Academy, Cordova, Tennessee

Jacqueline Nirode
Grand Care LLC, Franklin, Wisconsin

Jennifer Nizer
John Hopkins Bayview Medical Center Child
Development Center
Baltimore, Maryland

Julia Rand
Kids-Play, Uniontown, Ohio

Debbie Ritter
Small World Montessori Academy, Jensen Beach, Florida

Kathy Sarginson
ABCs of Children's Care, Foxboro, Ontario, Canada

Sherri Senter
National Pediatric Support Services, Irvine, California

Deborah Sheely
Tabitha Intergenerational Center, Lincoln, Nebraska

Elizabeth Shephard
Ready-Set-Grow, Inc., Auburn, Michigan

Pam Tuszynski
First Presbyterian Church Preschool
Hollywood, California

Linda Zager
Bloomington Developmental Learning Center
Bloomington, Indiana

Nine Steps to Fee Collections

Ideas from the Field

For more three decades *Exchange* has been surveying directors about fees and fee collections. From the ideas they have shared, we have developed nine steps that lead to effective and relatively painless collection of parent fees. Over the 30 years, what is remarkable, is how little the basic keys to success have changed. This 2010 version of the nine steps incorporates some new ideas, and much endorsement of classic principles, from Dan Lawler at Children's Choice Learning Centers in Dallas, Bob Siegel of Easter Seals in Chicago, and Fred Citron with Montgomery Early Learning Centers in Philadelphia. Directors who have shared their ideas in the past are listed at the end of the article.

Step 1
Spell Out Fee Policies on Day One

When enrolling a new family, explain to parents how the smooth operation of the center is dependent on all fees being paid on time. Fee payment schedules and procedures should be clearly presented verbally and then provided to parents in writing. This discussion should cover not only when and how to pay fees, but also what actions the center will take when payments are delinquent, and what steps parents can take in advance when they know they will have difficulty paying fees in a timely manner.

To avoid future misunderstandings and to underline the importance of these policies, many centers have parents sign a copy of the fee policies at enrollment. Since 98% of your parents make paying for quality child care on time a priority and don't want their care destabilized by late payments of others, you may want to have your fee policies endorsed by your parent group to add to their credibility.

Step 2
Keep in Close Touch with Parents

Parents in two situations are most likely to fall behind in paying fees. First, there are parents who are unhappy with the program and, therefore, feel little motivation to pay their fees on time. Second, families who are experiencing financial difficulties may be too embarrassed to ask for special consideration and, as a result, start falling behind.

One of the most effective steps you can take to avoid fee delinquencies is to maintain good relationships with parents. As director, you need to detect signs of disgruntlement early and deal with them before they get out of hand.

Likewise, if a director is on good terms with parents, they will feel more comfortable approaching him when they are in difficult straits. Directors have found that when they show understanding and work out a formal schedule of deferred fee payments at the outset of a problem, they are far more likely to experience success in collecting fees than when they only find out about a problem after parents start falling behind. In addition, working with parents in advance builds loyalty, whereas confronting parents in arrears often leads to resentment.

Many directors feel uncomfortable asking parents to pay their fees. If that is the case, you should focus on your pride in the service you are providing and thus not feel the least embarrassed about asking for remuneration. However, if it is just too hard for you to do this, designate someone else to take on this role, rather than continuing to do it without conviction.

Some centers offer a scholarship to reduce fees for families in crisis situations. However, for every dollar offered as a scholarship, there needs to be an equivalent dollar raised and set aside in a scholarship fund. Alternatively, some centers lower fees temporarily with the understanding (agreed to in writing) that the amount of the reduction will be made up over a set period of time when the crisis is over. Other centers assist families in securing assistance from public agencies, church groups, or other charitable organizations.

Step 3
Take the Pain Out of Paying

The easier you make it for parents to pay their fees, the less likely it is that you will run into problems. Here are steps some centers take to ease the paying:

■ Send out invoices with stamped return envelopes so parents can write out their checks and drop them in the mail, or better yet, send out invoices via email (saving printing and postage costs at the same time).

■ Offer parents the option of paying electronically — by credit card or via automated payments through their bank. Remember to factor the charges

you may incur for these conveniences into your budget.

■ Consider offering a discount for parents willing to pay well ahead. Some centers have had success with this; others avoid it as they see the discount as cutting into their revenues.

■ Have a locked box with a mail slot in the entryway so that parents can drop off their payments when they pick up their children.

Step 4
Collect Fees in Advance

Today, most centers require parents to pay for service before it is provided. This makes it easier for the center to keep ahead of the curve in paying its own bills. There is some variation in how advance payment policies are administered. Some centers collect fees as much as two months in advance; some collect fees the first day of every month; some collect fees on Wednesday for the following week's service; and some collect on Monday for that week's service.

From an administrative point of view, collecting fees for a month in advance is clearly advantageous — there are fewer payments to process and less opportunities for payments to be late.

However, for parents who have low-income jobs or who are paid on a weekly basis, paying a month in advance may be onerous — and predictably result in some late payments. Some centers have dealt with this dilemma by establishing a monthly fee policy and then working out biweekly or weekly payment plans for parents who can't pay on a monthly basis.

Step 5
Collect a Deposit

It is now common practice for centers to collect a security deposit equivalent to two weeks' or one month's fees. This fee is held and applied toward a parent's final fee payment. For centers, this deposit provides some assurance that a family will not leave owing fees.

However, in some communities it may be difficult, if not impossible, for parents to come up with a registration fee, advance tuition, and deposit at enrollment. Some centers allow parents to build up this 'escrow' a bit at a time for up to 8 weeks.

In instituting a deposit, be sure to investigate applicable state laws. Many states require that interest be paid to parents for deposits while that money is in the hands of the organization.

Step 6
Enforce Late Payment Penalties

Many centers have successfully discouraged late payments by charging penalties. Factors to keep in mind regarding payment penalties include:

- If you enact a payment penalty, enforce it automatically whenever there is a violation. If you enforce it only occasionally, you will send the message that parents don't need to worry about it.

- Consider a progressive penalty. If you have a one-time penalty, once the fine has been levied, there is little incentive to pay up. One center surveyed charges $1 for every day a payment is late, another charges $3 every two days.

- Whatever your penalty is, make sure it complies with state usury laws.

Step 7
Act Quickly

Quickness counts. As one director recounted, "I have found that I can avoid most serious problems by contacting delinquent parents immediately with a gentle reminder. Once a family falls more than a month behind, they seldom catch up."

For a parent who is late in paying only rarely, a written notice of delinquency will probably suffice.

However, for chronic late payers, immediate personal contact may be required. Those who make a practice of not paying bills on time are not likely to be influenced by form letters, no matter how threatening.

When negotiating with a parent over a late payment, it is important not to show anger or disrespect. Work at maintaining the dignity of the parent, and your own dignity will remain intact.

Step 8
Stop Providing Care

The ultimate penalty, when all remedies have been exhausted, is to stop providing services for families who fail to pay their fees. Most centers have seldom, if ever, found it necessary to exercise this option, as its mere threat is often sufficient to produce action.

Directors exercise varying degrees of patience before expelling a family. Most centers stop providing care after a parent falls a month behind, many after two weeks, and some as quickly as one week. Ideally, your deposit policy and your termination policy should be coordinated so that the deposit covers any unpaid balances upon termination.

Another safeguard against this step goes back to keeping in close touch with parents. If parents see a difficult stretch coming and let the director know, chances are that within reason, a plan can be worked out to stretch out payments. When a parent doesn't communicate and simply stops paying, this is a different matter.

Step 9
Take Legal Action

If a parent leaves your center owing you money, you have several approaches to consider to collect the balance due: you can continue pursuing payment on your own, you can turn the debt over to a collection agency, or you can sue in small claims court. Of these options, the first is least promising. If you haven't been able to convince a parent to pay while they were using your services, your chances of collecting after they leave are minimal.

Turning the account over to a collection agency is a painless alternative that may yield some results. Of course, you will have to share at least half of what is collected with the agency. And you need to be careful in selecting an agency because they will represent you in the community. If they use inappropriate collection techniques, this will reflect on your center.

Some centers have had success in suing parents in small claims court to recover unpaid fees. The advantage of this approach is that these courts operate informally: lawyers aren't required, both parties simply discuss the case with the judge. Directors have had much success in winning judgments in small claims court. One drawback of this approach is that winning a judgment does not guarantee payment. One director reported that in two decades they have taken parents to small claims court three times, won all three, and then never collected a penny. Other centers have found it necessary to go to the local sheriff to have judgments enforced.

Summary

While these nine steps may seem a bit on the extreme side, especially in a caring profession, they do avoid stress and loss of income. Centers that consistently enforce the early steps in the process rarely need to resort to the stronger measures. Centers that demonstrate their willingness to go all the way seldom experience losses. Most importantly, centers that work closely with parents, and support them in times of stress, are rewarded with strong parent loyalty.

Roger Neugebauer

Roger Neugebauer is founding publisher of *Exchange Magazine* and a co-founder of the World Forum Foundation.

Credits

The following center directors have contributed ideas to this article:

Judy Chosy
Smoky Row Children's Center, Powell, Ohio

Rose Dobkoski
Encompass Child Care, Green Bay, Wisconsin

Katheryne Chappell Drennon
Chappell Child Development Centers,
Jacksonville, Florida

Steve and Polly Eberhardt
FM Kirby Children's Center, Madison, New Jersey

Jane Flanagan
Flanagan's Pre-school
Conshohocken, Pennsylvania

Betsey Hale
Tender Loving Care, Pocatello, Idaho

Carla Horowitz
Calvin Hill Day Care Center
New Haven, Connecticut

Debra Imbriale
Dr. Goldberg Child Care Center
Westwood, New Jersey

Gail Laskowski
North Pocono Preschool, Moscow, Pennsylvania

Jill Hardwick Moore
Early Learning Center, Champaign, Illinois

Paula Olson
Hobson Coop Nursery School, Naperville, Illinois

Julia Rand
Kids-Play, Inc., Akron, Ohio

Roberta Recken
Fruit and Flower Day Nursery, Portland, Oregon

Leighan Rinker
Beginnings Child Care Center, Altantis, Florida

James Robertson
Plowshares Child Care Program,
Newtonville, Massachusetts

Linda Tynes, Enrichment Preschools,
Nashville, Tennessee

Gail and Doug Wiik, Breezy Point Day School,
Langhorne, Pennsylvania.

Surviving Tight Times

by Roger Neugebauer

"Daddy said tight times is why we all eat Mr. Bulk instead of cereals in little boxes."

In the children's book *Tight Times,* Barbara Shook Hazen portrays a little boy learning what financial crises are all about. Anyone who works in a child care center probably needs no such introduction. As in nearly all small businesses, financial ups and downs are a seemingly inevitable part of the organizational lifecycle. Leading one's center through tight times is an unwritten, yet central, aspect of all center owners' and directors' job descriptions.

However, if your center is now facing a financial crisis, you know that it will take more than serving Mr. Bulk instead of cereals in little boxes to pull through. It will require an array of aggressive actions as well as a large measure of tenacity. The following are some of the strategies recommended by small business experts to help for-profit and non-profit centers survive tight times.

Find Out What's Wrong

Neighborhood Child Care Center was broke. Director Jones, assuring everyone that this was just a temporary shortfall, whipped up enthusiasm for a major fundraising effort to pay off all the center's debts. Much to everyone's surprise, three months later Director Jones was again rounding up support for another fundraiser to help the center over another temporary crisis.

The reason that Director Jones' solutions failed is that she never grasped what the real problem was. If she had taken the time to analyze the situation, she would have found that the center's enrollment had been gradually, yet steadily, declining over the past six months. To solve the problem, Director Jones needed to focus her energy on building enrollments, not on organizing one-shot fundraisers.

For-profit center operators can experience a similar blindness to reality. I once observed, for example, a center owner who kept borrowing more and more money to get by 'temporary cash flow crises.' Unfortunately, he ignored the fact that over the years his expenses had crept up and up, while he had not raised parent fees significantly. In other words, his cash flow problems were not the result of temporary setbacks, but rather the fact that his budget was fatally flawed.

One of my favorite Monty Python skits is the "Changemakers." In this skit a banker explains their popular new program of providing customers with $1.05 in change for $1. When asked how the bank could possibly make money on this arrangement, he replied, "Oh, that's simple — volume."

When your center is running on empty, it is critical to find out why. You need to know if you are spending $1.05 for every $1 you take in.

You can't solve a problem until you know what's causing it. You should be able to get to the heart of the matter by finding answers to the following questions:

Are Your Income and Expenses in Line?

Often, as in the case of Neighborhood Child Care Center, directors' valiant efforts to keep their centers in the black only serve to mask a fundamental problem. This underlying problem frequently has to do with the bottom line. Sometimes centers keep encountering financial crises because their costs of doing business have inflated to the point where their fees (whether they are paid by parents or a public agency) are no longer high enough to cover expenses.

When tight times arrive, one of the first things a director should do is to perform a break-even analysis. The purpose of this analysis is to determine your break-even point — the fee level above which your center is making money and below which it is losing money.

If your fees are set well above your current break-even point, you know that you need to look elsewhere for the cause of your financial problems. If your fees are set close to, or below, the break-even point, this is undoubtedly a major cause (but sometimes not the only cause) of your problems.

Large organizations will need to perform separate break-even analyses for each distinct cost center. For example, if your organization has a separate fee scale for its infant, preschool, and afterschool components, each component should be analyzed as a separate cost center. If your organization provides care in more than one location, you may want to analyze each site as a separate cost center.

Following this approach you may find, for example, that your preschool and afterschool components are operating above their break-even points; but, your infant component is so far below break-even that it is dragging the whole operation under. Or, you may find that you are making money in certain locations, but losing it in others.

Is Your Enrollment Declining?

Go back and check your enrollment records for the past few months. Is your enrollment increasing, holding steady, or declining? How does it compare to the same time last year? If your enrollment is declining, you need to know why. There are three likely culprits, each requiring different actions on your part:

■ **Customer satisfaction may be eroding.** This can happen to any center, but it is a particularly common affliction in centers that have enjoyed extended periods of success. Month after month of long waiting lists and positive press coverage can lull any staff into taking parent satisfaction for granted. In the success mode it is easy to relax and fail to attend to all the details that make a difference in the program; to fall into a rut and become less creative and spontaneous; to stop taking the time to really communicate with parents.

Call up a random selection of your parents and talk to them informally about their attitudes about the program and where it is headed. Spend some time observing staff-child interactions in the classrooms and staff-parent interactions at drop-off and pick-up times. Talk to staff members to see if they have noticed any changes in the program.

If you find that your quality is slipping, you must act immediately to turn things around. Make restoring customer confidence your top priority. Give program improvement high profile in staff meetings, written communications, and in frequent personal tours of the classrooms. Keep in touch with parents to see if the results are being noticed.

- **Competition may be heating up.** Five years ago you may have been the only show in town. But today, there may be a number of centers that are chipping away at your customer base.

Conduct exit interviews when parents withdraw their children from your center. Do follow-up calls to parents who made initial inquiries about your center but did not enroll their children. Find out why parents are electing to place their children in centers other than your own.

Once you determine what your competitors' advantages are, you need to decide how to respond. For example, if you are losing customers because the other centers' prices are lower, you may choose to lower your prices as well. However, in doing so you may dilute your quality to the point where you drive away your firmest supporters. An alternative might be to raise your prices and gear your program more specifically towards families that are willing and able to pay for high quality.

- **Your market may be changing.** Demographic shifts may be occurring in your community that are impacting the demand for your services. Maybe the neighborhoods around your center are aging, so there just aren't as many preschool children as there used to be. Maybe your neighborhoods are being overrun by Yuppies who are looking for a glitzier program than you provide. Maybe household incomes aren't keeping pace with inflation, and families can't afford you anymore. Maybe your traditional funding bases, such as the United Way or the Junior League, no longer see child care as a priority.

If your market is changing dramatically, you may be fighting an uphill battle. Temporary infusions of cash may keep the program afloat for a few months, but at some point you will need to face some tough decisions. It may be necessary to change your location, to substantially reduce your operations, or maybe even to call it quits.

Are Your Receivables Mounting?

Caring is what running a center is all about. Sometimes, however, a director can become so concerned about caring for people that she avoids pressing them when they get behind in paying their fees.

Take a look at your accounts receivable report. Has the bottom line been building up from month to month? Is your laxity in collecting overdue fees starting to undermine the financial stability of the center? If there is a problem developing in the receivables area, you need to respond quickly and firmly. The longer you delay in responding, the more you will end up writing off as bad debts.

Monitor Cash Flow Diligently

Once you have discovered the source of the problem, you need to determine how serious it is. The best way to do this is by preparing a cash flow analysis. Such an analysis enables you to predict when your center won't have enough cash in the bank to pay its bills and how big the deficit will be.

Routinely, cash flow projections should be made on a monthly basis. However, when tight times arrive, it is advisable to monitor cash flowing in and out of your center on a weekly basis. This will enable you to pinpoint most accurately the weeks where money will be the tightest, as well as those weeks where you may have a little breathing room. This information is extremely helpful because it gives you a clear picture of the extent of the problem.

As you proceed through a rocky period, you will find that the weekly cash flow projections are also an invaluable tool for working on solutions. By keeping the projections up-to-date, you can closely monitor your progress, or lack thereof, in dealing with the problem. You can test out various proposed solutions to see their impact. For example, you could hypothesize, "What if we raised fees in the infant room by $2 per week?," plug the new income projections into your cash flow, and see how that impacts the bottom line week by week.

Trim the Fat

When your financial ink turns red, your first thought is often, "Where can we cut back?" This is, in theory, the reasonable thing to do. But, in practice, it may not do the trick. After you exempt those expenditures you are contractually bound to, those you can't cut without a corresponding reduction in income, and those that would detract noticeably from program quality or staff morale, you often are left with little fat to trim. Nonetheless, in tight times you do need to analyze the savings potential in each line item in the budget to see if there are some real opportunities to absorb some of the red ink. The most effective way to do this is to list the monthly allocation for each line item and then to calculate the percent each line item would have to be cut in order to save $100 (divide 100 by the amount of each line item). A quick review of the resulting figures will identify those areas where significant cuts can be made without a dramatic negative impact on the program.

Slow Outflow of Cash

If cutting costs doesn't seem to be the answer, deferring costs is another approach that can help an ailing cash flow. If planned major expenditures (such as resurfacing the playground) can be delayed for weeks or months, this can often help more than making painful budget cuts.

At the outset of a crunch period, you should also consider meeting with your major creditors to see if they would be willing to extend your credit. If you owe a sizable amount to a bank, for example, you should explain your financial dilemma and request a restructuring of the note. While bankers will grunt and groan and make all sorts of our-hands-are-tied statements, basically they will do what they have to do to get their money back. If they drive you out of business by holding you to the original payment schedule, they stand to be the losers. (See box on the following page, "How to Keep the Wolves from the Door" for more thoughts on how to deal with people trying to collect money from you.)

Speed the Inflow of Cash

Looking now at the other end of the cash flow equation, red ink can also be combatted by speeding up the rate at which money owed to you is collected. There are a number of steps you can take in this regard:

- **Invoice promptly**. You can't expect people to pay you on time if you are tardy in billing them.

- **Reward early payers.** Announce a discount for paying within the first few days of a billing cycle, or an even larger discount for paying in advance.

- **Punish late payers**. Announce penalties (in line with state regulations on interest charges) for late payments, and enforce them religiously.

- **Stay on top of overdue fees**. Don't let late payers get very far behind without letting them know you are on their case. Directors have found that if families get more than three months behind in their payments they are much more likely to drop-out than to pay up. By getting in touch with families falling behind early and working out short-term, spread out repayment plans, you are much more likely both to retain them as your customers and to eventually receive payment in full.

- **Expedite other income**. If you have been awarded a grant by a local business or United Way, see if you can receive the money early, or secure a temporary loan from a bank in anticipation of this income. See if you can get the state to pay you monies they owe you early or on time (we had to throw this one in for laughs). If you have an annual fundraiser, check into scheduling it earlier this year.

Explore New Income Sources

Pumping new currency into your center's money veins can also be invigorating. When a cash flow crisis is on the horizon, you could call a meeting of key people within your organization who have a stake in its success, as well as resourceful people from outside who care about your organization. Use this as an occasion to brainstorm all kinds of ways your center could generate new money. The possibilities come in all shapes and sizes:

■ **Raising fees** — for everyone, for new enrollees only, or for certain cost centers.

How to Keep the Wolves from the Door

How do you keep your creditors satisfied when times are tight? Here are some pointers:

- **Goodwill is money in the bank.** Anyone with a thick enough skin can stave off creditors indefinitely. However, while a totally hard-nosed approach may help you survive a crisis, what price will you pay? If you alienate everyone you buy services and supplies from during tight times, they may refuse to do business with you when the good times arrive. Even when the creditors are pressing hard, you should strive to salvage some degree of goodwill by treating them in a respectful, business-like manner.

- **Creditors don't like surprises.** When you know you are going to have a problem meeting a financial obligation, call the creditor in advance to let him know you've got a problem. This demonstrates that you take your obligations seriously and gives him time to adjust his cash flow projections. A creditor will be much less conciliatory if he has to call you after your account becomes delinquent.

- **Honesty is still the best policy.** Popular myth has it that you keep creditors at bay through a series of deceptions — "Haven't we already paid that? I'll have to check our records." Such transparent ruses tend to aggravate creditors and motivate them to become more aggressive in their actions against you. Honestly explain that your center is experiencing a severe, yet temporary, cash flow problem and that you will pay what you owe as quickly as you can.

- **Promise only what you can deliver.** Creditors will want you to commit to a repayment schedule. Unless you are really certain about improving prospects in the near future, avoid making specific commitments. If you fail to meet a new due date, you are going to double a creditor's frustration.

- **Less is more.** Try to make small partial payments periodically to all creditors, rather than paying in full the ones that scream the loudest. Even a trickle of cash will let creditors know your center is still in business and that you are serious about paying your bills.

- **Don't blame the victim.** Tight times can be incredibly trying, so when a creditor calls and harasses you for his money, it is very easy to become angry and vent all your frustrations. You must keep in mind, however, that the reason he is pressing you is that he provided something to you in good faith and now you have violated the agreement. He has every right to press you. If you find yourself becoming upset by what a creditor is saying when he calls, don't lash out emotionally. Tell him you will call back with an answer, and then wait until you have cooled off and developed a logical response.

■ **Boosting enrollment** — turning around declining enrollments or over-enrolling to maintain nearly full capacity.

■ **Expanding the program** — adding an afterschool component, adding two more children to each current classroom, opening a new center.

■ **One-shot activities** — dinners, fairs, house tours, raffles, auctions, cookbook sales, and jog-a-thons.

■ **One-shot appeals** — annual membership drives, jog-a-thons, direct mail solicitation campaigns, corporate appeals, one-on-one appeals.

■ **Annual events** — taking a one-shot activity or appeal and repeating it every year.

■ **Ongoing activities** — parenting seminars, convention child care, weekend activity classes, computer classes, family kitchens, thrift shops.

■ **Grants-in-aid** — foundation grants, United Way funding, public funding, local grants.

■ **Loans** — from banks, the SBA, local business people, Aunt Emma.

■ **Investments** — forming a partnership, securing outside investors, selling shares. Once you have a long list of possibilities, evaluate each one in terms of the following criteria:

• **How soon will it generate income?** If you are going to be $3,000 in the red in three weeks, and the idea under review won't kick in for two months, keep looking.

• **Is it cost effective?** Estimate how much income the idea would generate, how much it would cost to carry it out, and divide the balance by the number of person-hours required to carry it out. This computation will tell you how much profit you will generate for every hour of effort. Successful fundraisers generate anywhere from $25 to $200 per hour. If a project will produce less than $10 per hour of effort, think twice before giving the go-ahead.

• **Do we possess appropriate resources?** In their popular book, *In Search of Excellence*, Thomas J. Peters and Robert H. Waterman, Jr. observe that one of the traits of successful businesses is that they stick to their knitting, they know what they are good at, and don't go far afield in developing new products or services. In evaluating new income-generating thrusts for a child care center, you need to question whether this is an activity that builds on your current strengths (where you have people — paid or volunteer — with appropriate skills, space, and materials that are appropriate, and an established reputation in the area) or one which would require your organization to start from scratch.

• **What is the likelihood of success?** During a financial crisis, the time of the director and other key center people needs to be focused exclusively on high-impact activities. Time wasted on nonproductive or marginally productive activities could spell the difference between surviving and failing. Putting together a prospectus to attract investors can take weeks and weeks of top management time, as can putting together a grant proposal for a foundation. Yet in both cases the likelihood of success is extremely low. Before committing that kind of time to an activity, you need to do some preliminary research, which assures you that you are not diverting much needed energy into a dead-end project.

• **What are the side-effects of the idea?** If we raise our fees, will we lose half our customers? If we start another center, will we have to pull too many of our best teachers away from our existing center? If we attract an investor, will we have to turn over too much control to a third party? If we get a United Way grant, will we be bogged down in their red tape? If we get a loan from Aunt Emma, will we feel guilty until we pay her back?

After weighing all these issues, you should be able to identify several hot ticket income generators. You can now throw these into the hopper with all your other potential cash flow solutions — ideas for speeding up income, deferring expenses, and cutting expenses. From among all of these possibilities you will need to construct a combination of actions that will pull you out of debt.

Hang in There

Tight times can cause more than a financial strain. Eventually they cause excruciating emotional and physical strain for the leaders of the organization. Al Masini has observed that nothing raises the energy reservoir like success and nothing depletes it like failure. Working hard on a venture that is taking off is exhilarating, but slaving away on a venture mired in red ink is enervating.

Worrying about money for weeks on end is mentally and socially taxing. After awhile you eat, sleep, and drink cash flow. All you can think or talk about is whether you can meet the payroll on Friday. You end up being a not very fun person to be around.

Having creditors insult you, swear at you, and threaten you gets to be a drag. Friendships turn sour as you fall behind on financial obligations. As Orson Welles remarked, "When you're down and out, something always turns up — and it's usually the noses of your friends."

What often determines whether an organization survives a financial crisis is the tenacity of the persons at the top — their ability to endure all the strain and work effectively toward a solution. Actress Helen Hayes once commented that talent and ability are not enough: "Nothing is any good without endurance."

Not only must the leaders of the center hang in there, but they also must maintain a positive public attitude. Although your inner self may be crying out for pity, you can't afford to cry on the shoulders of your customers or your staff. If parents get the message that your center is on the rocks, they will start looking for a more stable child care arrange-

ment. Staff, likewise, may start abandoning a ship that they believe is sinking.

This is not to say you should deceive parents and staff into thinking everything is rosy. If you don't say anything, rumors of all sorts will start flying as soon as the first signs of red ink appear. When you are about to experience an extended dry spell, you should inform staff and parents in a businesslike manner that cash flow difficulties call for some careful budgeting over the coming weeks. But assure them that the long-term projections are positive, so that any inconvenience will be temporary.

Then, when good times arrive, throw a party.

Don't Let it Happen Again

After you mount a prodigious effort and pull through a financial crisis, it is easy to succumb to traumatic amnesia — you forget about how bad things were. You are so relieved to have survived that you let your guard down and relax too long. And before you know it, the grocer is calling to find out when he can expect payment on his overdue invoice. To avoid this cycle:

- Do keep your finger on the financial pulse of the organization.

- Don't let up on closely monitoring the cash flow.

- Do periodically check your break-even points to make sure you are not involuntarily becoming a charitable institution.

- Do develop an annual budget and monitor your performance monthly.

- Don't confuse growth with profits. Remember, just because your organization is getting bigger, it is not necessarily doing better on the bottom line.

- Don't live it up too soon. After your checkbook shows a positive balance, don't rush out and make all the purchases you put off.

■ Do work to reestablish a solid credit rating. Pay your bills promptly. Supply your banker and funders with monthly balance sheets and income statements. Apply for an adequate line of credit after an extended period of solid financial performance. If you are a non-profit, you will likewise find it easier to ask for support from funders when you are operating in the black. Charitable donors are much more inclined to invest in vision and vitality than they are to cover debt and dysfunction.

■ Do stay close to your customers. Don't get so pre-occupied with the numbers that you forget who is paying the bills. Stay tuned to their concerns, their needs, their changing means.

■ And, last but not least, don't make the same mistake twice. As Ted S. Frost suggests, "If you're going to get yourself into financial trouble again, at least have enough class to think up some different way of doing it."

Roger Neugebauer

Roger Neugebauer is founding publisher of *Exchange Magazine* and a co-founder of the World Forum Foundation.

Establishing and Managing a Tuition Aid Program

by Teresa Vast

The primary goal of a tuition aid program is to help families enroll and keep their children in your center. Tuition aid revenue can also improve your center's financial stability and boost quality. This article explores some of the basic issues in establishing and managing a tuition assistance program — target groups, sources of aid, determining need, and whether to use an external financial aid service.

Tuition Aid Helps Families AND Centers

As an early childhood administrator you know that financial barriers prevent many families from enrolling their children in your center. Among participating families, late and missed payments tell you that many parents struggle to pay the tuition and fees.

Moreover, since tuition revenue comprises an average 87% of the typical center budget (Cost, Quality & Child Outcomes Study Team, 1995), low or fluctuating enrollment can threaten your center's financial viability and the quality of your program.

Most directors strive to set prices at affordable levels, often relying on subsidies of donated space, goods and services, and on the willingness of staff to accept low wages. But even these 'bargain' prices are higher than many can afford. Public child care subsidies help some families pay, but many states' authorized payment rates fall short of the tuition and fees (Adams & Snyder, 2003).

To increase financial stability, many providers seek funds from private sector sources to bridge the gap between what families can pay and what it costs to produce a high-quality program. One approach is to raise funds for a need-based tuition aid program. Setting clear goals and guidelines for such a program will help you both in raising the funds and in equitably awarding aid to families.

Target Groups

In establishing and managing a tuition aid fund, the most fundamental question is "Who do you want to assist?" The answer will depend largely on your program's mission, the communities you serve, and the resources available. While some programs focus resources on the families with the lowest-income and greatest need, others reach out to families with moderate income who also have financial need. Additional goals, such as increasing diversity, can also be addressed within the framework of need-based aid. Since need usually far exceeds aid resources, priorities should be established to ensure aid is distributed in such a way that the purposes are fulfilled.

Some potential target groups include:

Families of low-income means...

- who do not meet the eligibility criteria to qualify for publicly-funded child care assistance.

- who receive child care assistance, but must make a larger co-payment than they can afford, either because the child care eligibility formula does not reflect basic living expenses or the rate does not reflect real early care and education prices.

- who meet eligibility requirements for public child care assistance via a voucher or admission in a contracted center or enrollment in Head Start, but are placed on a waiting list or turned away.

- whose children may lose early learning opportunities when a parent loses a job and employment-related child care benefits.

Moderate- and middle-income gap group families...

- who are ineligible, based on income, for publicly-funded child care assistance, but do not have the financial resources to pay for high-quality early care and education.

When is Reduced or Free Tuition not Aid?

If a tuition discount or free enrollment is not based on financial need, it should be accounted for separately in the center's budget. Examples include reduced or waived tuition provided as employee benefits (a personnel expense), and sibling discounts available to families regardless of demonstrated financial need (a marketing expense).

Sources of Tuition Aid

Once purposes for tuition aid have been established, you have a strong basis for raising needed funds. A community foundation or fund development professional can help you identify promising charitable sources and devise a strategy to meet your program's revenue goals.

While not all revenue sources or strategies are appropriate to every type of program nor are available in every area, potential sources for tuition aid include:

- charitable grants from community or private foundations or corporations.

- contributions from the United Way or community service clubs.

- gifts from wealthy individuals familiar with your program.

- commercial enterprises operated as a subsidiary.

- fundraising activities, such as direct-mail appeals to alumni families and community supporters; special events such as concerts, auctions; and occasional or regular sales of specialty items and merchandise.

- endowment income: Some programs create an endowment fund to generate interest income, a strategy long-used by colleges, universities, and many private K-12 schools. Once established and adequately funded, an endowment can provide a stable source of revenue for tuition aid.

Finally, tuition revenue itself can be a source of financial aid, usually as a supplement to other sources. Some programs include aid as a standard budget expense category, designating a portion of revenue (e.g. 5%) to the tuition aid line item in accordance with their mission and purposes (e.g. to establish a diverse school community).

Managing the Tuition Aid Program

Raising the money is but one step in getting tuition aid to those who need it. Policies and procedures that address who will manage the fund and how the program is implemented are also essential.

Staffing. It takes time and diverse skills to oversee and manage a tuition aid fund. Large and multi-site programs are more likely to hire staff to administer financial aid, while small programs are more likely to add these responsibilities to the director's role. In either case, the added expense should be reflected in the budget.

Financial aid staff needs communication and people skills to advise and counsel parents. They also need math and computation skills for reviewing applications and tax returns. They have to keep an eye on the big picture of the purposes of the aid and also pay attention to details in tracking data and keeping records. Professionalism is a must in dealing with sensitive and confidential information.

Policies. Written policies and procedures form the foundation of the tuition aid program. They help you to administer the funds impartially and with confidentiality. They must be clear and fair, so that parents, staff, and funders can trust the process and the results. Policies and procedures should address: staff and volunteer roles and responsibilities, outreach activities, application forms and processes, methods for calculating financial need and ability to pay, guidelines for equitably distributing aid, and an appeals process. Guidelines for record keeping, protection of privacy, and use of data should also be included.

Determining Need and Awarding Aid

Early care and education programs are often unprepared for the delicate task of reviewing families' financial information and assessing their ability to pay. The absence of a uniform national method (like those used in college financial aid) adds to the challenge. Many programs have devised sliding scales as a rough measure of ability to pay, but these can vary widely, even within a single community.

As a director, you want to have confidence in your methods and be able to demonstrate effective use of limited funds. Potential contributors may also be interested in knowing that you base aid decisions on valid assumptions.

Colleges, universities, and many private K-12 schools rely on standard methods and forms and an external financial aid service. Their process is a useful guide. Three key questions outline the major steps: What is the family able to pay? How much aid is needed to close the gap between what the family can pay and the program's tuition price? What portion of the family's financial need can you meet with available tuition aid resources?

■ How much can the family pay toward your center's tuition and fees?

To ensure that families are treated equitably and that limited funds are wisely awarded, a uniform method based on sound economic principles should be used to calculate what a family can reasonably contribute. The formula and process should consider family size, income, assets, and special circumstances reported by applicants on a form you provide, verified with tax returns and other documents. After deducting standard allowances for basic necessities (e.g. food, shelter, taxes), families can be expected to pay a portion of any remaining income.

One option is to rely on an external financial aid service for the forms, method, and financial need analysis. For more information about issues in determining families' ability to pay, see *Learning Between Systems: Adapting Higher Education Financing Methods to Early Care and Education* (Vast, 2001).

■ What is the financial need of the family?

Once you have determined how much families can pay for early care and education, calculating their need for financial assistance is a matter of simple math:

Tuition and fees
– Expected family contribution
= Need

■ **What portion of the family's financial need can you meet?**

Distributing limited funds is a balancing act. The amount you award to each family will depend on your available tuition aid funds, your program's priorities, the amount each family needs, and the relative need of all families who qualify for assistance. When need outpaces aid, a common method of rationing involves meeting a percentage of need.

Due to the sensitivity of award decisions, it is wise to have a committee or volunteer oversight group to consider the relative need of the various applicants in relation to the program's purposes and priorities. However, all who have access to a family's financial information must maintain confidentiality.

In-house or External Financial Aid Service?

In contrast to other levels of education, no financial aid service currently exists that is geared specifically to early care and education programs and the families they serve. Perhaps this will change in the future when social and financial investments in early care and education expand to match the importance of the early years. Public and private funders may eventually demand the same level of reliability and accountability that financial aid methods now provide in higher education and many private K-12 schools.

There are good reasons to consider using an external financial aid service rather than attempting to handle everything in-house (see sidebar above). But there are also disadvantages in using available services. This was clearly demonstrated in a recent experiment

---

Why Use a Financial Aid Service?

- Research-based method produces reliable results for making fair aid decisions.

- Eliminates need to develop a valid method, create forms, and perform complex calculations.

- Additional training and support is available to service subscribers.

Why Use an In-house Financial Aid Method?

- Your program has developed forms and methods using valid and current economic research and resources.

- Your program has dedicated staff with financial aid skills.

- Your program has access to training and support from a volunteer or consultant with financial aid expertise

---

in Hawaii in which two foundations provided tuition aid to a dozen preschools with a requirement that all families use the same financial aid application form. Key to this approach was the availability of a third-party method and processing system. The School and Student Service for Financial Aid (SSS) was used for the foundations' experiment.

A project of the National Association of Independent Schools (NAIS), SSS provides financial aid applications and processing services for over 2,300 K-12 schools nationwide; only a handful of early care and education programs currently subscribe to the service. Parents complete a uniform application, send it to SSS, and the schools named by the parents receive the results, including the 'estimated family contribution.' The schools use the information they receive in calculating need and awarding aid. Costs of the service are paid through annual fees from participating schools ($125) and application fees paid by families ($20). Families with low incomes are given fee waivers.

Preschools that used SSS gave mixed reviews of their experience:

Advantages:

■ The form and process was helpful in setting up a new tuition aid program.

■ Using the service saved staff time in creating forms and calculating income.

■ The SSS calculations provided results that could be trusted — a useful tool for determining need.

■ The 'estimated family contribution' was useful in prioritizing need and making award decisions.

■ The impartiality of an objective third-party process improved parent-director relationships.

Disadvantages:

■ The parents' financial form was intimidating and difficult for many applicants.

■ Staff had to provide extensive assistance to some applicants, particularly families with low incomes.

■ The form includes unnecessary questions for families with limited resources.

■ The processing time was too long for the school and parents.

■ The services are geared to 9-month school calendars and limited application periods.

■ The forms and process were more labor intensive than programs' usual practices.

Mark Mitchell, vice president for financial aid services at NAIS, acknowledges that there is room for improvement in making the SSS application more user-friendly and shaping the service to meet the needs of early care and education programs. He notes NAIS plans for a flexible online form that would simplify the process for applicants with low income and few assets, but still capture all necessary data from those with more complex finances. For additional information about SSS, contact Mark Mitchell at (202) 973-9766 or mitchell@nais.org or visit www.nais.org.

A different kind of 'third-party' approach is used by some centers that serve predominantly families with low incomes receiving public assistance. Rather than submitting families to another application process, they rely on government-administered needs tests. For example, if the family qualifies for a particular level of child care assistance that falls short of the tuition price, the program uses private tuition aid funds to make up the difference between the tuition price and the combined total of the family co-payment and publicly-funded voucher.

Regardless of whether an in-house process or external financial aid service is used, the key is to ensure that aid awards are equitable, based on sound data and reliable methods that clearly establish need.

Looking to the Future

The concept of a community-based financial aid 'hub' has sparked interest among advocates nationwide. A centralized financial aid agency, perhaps co-located with a child care resource and referral agency or other family-oriented services, would be a resource for families seeking tuition assistance and could also serve as an external financial aid office for area providers (Vast, 2001). Concentrating expertise and services in a community agency would reduce the burden on providers and increase access for parents — without the stigma of welfare. This could be especially important as funding eventually increases and eligibility for aid expands.

In the meantime, you can develop your center's tuition aid fund. Using the steps outlined here, you could fine-tune your methods and processes, or experiment with a new approach, such as using an external financial aid service. Innovative center directors seeking to maximize their use of available funds and resources could even form a network to jointly establish a financial aid service that is customized for early care and education and geared to their needs.

References

Cost, Quality & Child Outcomes Study Team. (1995). *Cost Quality, and Child Outcomes in Child Care Centers*, Public Report (2nd edition). Denver: Department of Economics, University of Colorado at Denver, p. 44, table 5.1.

Adams, G., & Snyder, K. (February 2003). "Essential but Often Ignored: Child Care Providers in the Subsidy System." Occasional Paper Number 63, *Assessing the New Federalism*. Washington, DC: The Urban Institute.

Vast, T. (July 2001). *Learning between systems: Adapting higher education finance methods to early care and education, Final Project Report*. Indianapolis, IN: Lumina Foundation for Education, pp. 27–33.

Teresa Vast

Teresa Vast is an independent early childhood consultant who specializes in policy research and analysis, planning, and program development. Her projects focus primarily on system financing and career development systems. Teresa has done extensive research on adapting higher education financing methods to early care and education, and has designed and implemented several tuition aid programs. She received her bachelor's and master's degrees in human development from Pacific Oaks College.

Staffing at the Child Care Center

by Lori Harris

You are nearing the end of a really promising interview for the lead teacher position in your infant/toddler program and you ask if there are any questions. You hear the dreaded words, "I can't remember if you said what the hours were, but I really would rather work early and get out in the middle of the afternoon." (The hours you are looking for are 10 am–6 pm.) What are you going to do now?

Staffing and scheduling are just one part of a center director's job. Most of us do not give it the time and attention it needs. It is a task that requires organizational skills and interpersonal skills to put together a staffing pattern that works for the people and the center. Many years ago when I was starting a new center, I was determined to find a way to get highly qualified staff without spending a fortune. I searched for information and found a couple of articles, but nothing that helped me look at patterns from different perspectives. I started to do my own work on patterns, budgets, and qualifications. Over the years I have learned a lot, both from personal experience and talking to directors from all over the United States. I have pulled together some of those discoveries below. I am using the term 'director' to identify the person who puts together the schedule even though it may be someone other than the director in some situations.

Scheduling Tips

Count the Children

The director must know how many children are present, when they are present, and where they are in order to schedule staff appropriately. Many programs have parents sign their children in and out — but not all programs require parents to note the time of arrival and departure when signing in and out. If you do require times, your counts are nearly done! If not, you will have to dedicate some time to it. The count should be done whenever there is a substantial change in enrollment. (See Appendix B on page 96 for the count form.) For many programs that would be September and January and perhaps June or July. It is important to wait a couple of weeks after any enrollment changes to let families 'settle in' before you do the count. You do not want to staff for peak enrollment unless that enrollment is going to continue throughout the year. That way, you will be getting the most accurate times for departure and arrival. Four more points to remember are:

■ The count should be done for every group of children throughout the entire day for one week. Make sure to note the earliest arrival time during the week and the earliest times you need a second staff person, as well as the earliest you can let a second person go and the latest departure time. The idea is to make sure you are not understaffed for any part of the day and that you are not over-staffed for major parts of the day either.

- Pick a time for the count that does not reflect a temporary peak enrollment. You may have to bring in some extra staff at peak times if they are very different from the expected enrollment for most of the year. That may be preferable to being overstaffed most of the year.

An example of a peak enrollment is a summer camp program. At my program we run a full-day kindergarten program during the school year and a summer camp program in the summer. The child summer camp program is larger than the kinder-garten program and has different staffing needs.

- Beginnings and ends of the day are important. Count every 15 minutes for the first and last hour-and-a-half your center is open, every half-hour until all children arrive and when they start to leave, and hourly during the middle of the day when all the children are present. Make note if there are a number of children who come and go in the middle of the day. While counting every 15 minutes during arrival and departure may seem extreme, it can make a difference in the coverage.

- Infant and toddler nap times should be noted, since staffing needs should be determined based on the times when all children are present and awake. For example, staff breaks should be sched-uled for sleeping times, not when all children are awake. This is not to say that staff:child ratios should be out of compliance at any time — even during breaks. If you use a substitute to cover breaks, it is better to rotate that person in during naps than when all children are awake.

Build the Schedule

Once the count of children is established, the sched-ule can be built. For the purpose of this article we will be using the terms teacher and assistant teacher.

Staff roles at child care centers are identified by different terminology across the country. Some states use the term 'lead teacher' to indicate a staff mem-ber with higher qualifications than the ones called 'teachers,' while others use the term 'lead teachers' to mean the primary teacher in every classroom. Others use the term 'teacher' for anyone in charge of a classroom.

Some states create three roles: the assistant or aide, the teacher, and a better-qualified teacher (called by a variety of names). In centers in those states, all class-rooms have to have a qualified teacher, as defined in licensing; but larger centers are required to have a certain number or percentage of teachers with still more coursework and/or experience. Not all teachers must meet these higher requirements; usually some number based on the size of the center. Aides are typically employed on a provisional basis, without pre-service qualifications.

For the assisting staff other than aides, some states use 'associate teacher,' others use 'teacher assistant.' The qualifications for these assisting roles can be quite complex and varied as well. For the purposes of this document, a teacher is someone who is qualified to supervise a group of children and another less qualified adult. That teacher has had some course-work in early childhood education and experience on the job. The assistants are people who may have some knowledge of early childhood but would typically not be permitted to work with a group of children by themselves.

The following 13 points should be noted:

- **A qualified person should open and close the center.** That person could be the director or other administrator, or a well-qualified teacher. Arrival and departure of the children is very important. Not only can it be a difficult transition time, but also it is the only time some parents are in the center. You want your most experienced and capable staff on hand when the children arrive and depart. There are usually plenty of qualified people in the morning for drop off; care should be taken to ensure qualified people at the end of the day as well. Some centers have a 'welcome room' for the first arrivals, and a 'goodbye room' for those few who stay later than the others. These centers are careful to assure qualified staffing for these rooms, so that the children are engaged with each other in activities, and are not just waiting.

■ **There should be a qualified teacher for every group of children.** Early childhood training and experience is critical to the quality of the care the children receive. The teacher must be able to plan and coordinate the group activity, so she must be able to monitor individual children and the group as a whole. As you recruit staff, use your own standards. The quality of the service you want to bring to children and their families depends on your staff. Licensing standards and accreditation criteria give you some ideas; you need to add your own criteria and standards to find the people who will ensure your quality.

When recruiting teachers it is also important to reflect the diversity of the center and the community in the staff. Reflecting the diversity means very different things across the United States. The questions to ask are the same, however: Can the staff speak the languages of the families? Do they know the various cultures? Can they communicate with families? Do they provide visible role models for the children?

■ **There should be at least two staff in the center at all times.** Some believe there should be two people in every classroom at all times in order to ensure the safety of the children. This goal is not financially realistic for most programs, but it is important that you never leave a person alone with children in the building. In larger programs, the two adults do not have to be together in the same location in the building. It is important, however, that they are able to communicate with one another.

■ **Be careful of numbers of adults and supervision responsibilities.** It is critical to maintain a staff:child ratio that ensures a high-quality safe environment for children. While it is important to make sure there are enough adults, it is possible to have too many adults with a group of children as well. This seems to be especially true in infant and toddler rooms, when adults can seem to outnumber the children even when they don't.

In addition, teachers who are supervising other staff should not be expected to directly supervise more than two other adults while working with the children. Those adults include apprentices, assistants, and volunteers who need to be monitored. Staff that are counted in the ratios are limited in many states to employees who are qualified for their role. In those states, high school students or others who work limited hours or may have little or no early childhood knowledge, can volunteer or work at the center, but are not counted as staff in the staff:child ratio requirement.

■ **Overlap the staff schedules.** There should be at least a 15-minute overlap of shifts to ease the transition for children and adults. The shifts should not all change at the same time; at least one staff person should be staying through the shift change. The overlap benefits the parents by assuring that the staff have opportunities to share information about the children to pass along to the parent. It benefits the organization by its impact on the dynamics of the team. It is particularly important with any group of children who sleep at will (infants and some toddlers) to be aware of children's schedules and then plan for coverage accordingly.

■ **Think about using split shifts.** A split shift is one that schedules a staff member in the early morning, and also in the late afternoon and evening. In the middle of the day, the employee does not work at the center. Split shifts can be very helpful to parents when they are scheduled to accommodate the beginning and the end of the day in that parents get to talk to the same person about their child. Everyone on staff won't be willing to work a split shift. Capitalize on the ones who are willing and anxious to do it. If a split shift is used, regular check-in with that employee is essential. You will want to allow them to change their schedule when it becomes a hardship for any reason.

■ **Think about 10-hour shifts**. Some programs schedule staff for four days of 10-hour shifts. This can work particularly well under specialized enrollment situations, for instance when there are many part-time families and one day per week has low enough enrollment to warrant a reduction of staff. It has been my experience that while most staff like the idea of 10-hour shifts in theory and can keep them up for a time, they tire of the long days eventually and the quality of care suffers. Effectiveness drops off dramatically during hours 8, 9, and 10. Be careful using this staffing strategy.

■ **Consider a policy regarding continuity of care**. There are many different ways centers implement this concept. For some centers it means that the caregiver stays with the children as they move from one age group to another. Children are not promoted to a new group as soon as they reach a certain age. For other centers it means that the caregivers work 10-hour days to minimize the number of staff involved with the children. For yet other centers, it means assigning a primary caregiver who knows their primary children better than any of the other caregivers in the room.

Some centers use a primary caregiver who stays with the child from infancy through preschool. Others have one primary caregiver when the child is an infant and toddler and another when the child is in preschool. Regardless of the model, the idea is to minimize the number of times a child has to establish a new primary relationship with an adult outside his or her families.

■ **Schedule breaks between every four hours of work**. Labor laws vary from state to state. Some require that every employee be allowed a 15- to 20-minute break for every four hours of work, while others exempt those who work with young children. A 15- to 20-minute break should be the norm in every center regardless of the labor laws. People need time to shut down and regroup in any

job; but it is critically important when working in a child care center — where the children depend on the staff for their positive experiences.

■ **Schedule planning time every day for every staff person**. Classroom staff needs time away from children and the classroom to plan. They need a place with adult-sized chairs and tables and resources appropriate to the age groups in the center. While a daily planning time may seem impossible to schedule, it is easier in some ways than trying to give everyone one time per week. (See sample schedules in Appendix A.) If planning time is scheduled every day, but a day has to be skipped for whatever reason, it is not as critical as skipping a once-a-week planning time.

It is important to allow every staff person from lead teachers to assistant teachers some time to plan. The assistant teachers add a perspective of their own, which can be of great value. I believe the buy-in gained by including assistant teachers results in longer retention and higher job satisfaction, and a greater willingness to pursue further training. Make sure to give the same time and access to the infant and toddler staff — it requires just as much planning and preparation for that age group of children as it requires for older children.

■ **Remain objective when assigning coverage to groups of children**. Nothing wreaks havoc in a schedule like personal relationships. A director who feels obligated to give staff the schedules they favor can create a disaster if those preferences do not match the children's schedules. Once the count is done, the director knows when and where staff is needed. The schedule should be determined by children's needs, not adult needs.

Do you schedule with no names, but then add the names to the shifts based on staff preferences? For example, if you have a teacher who wants to work 7 am to 3 pm, you give him a morning shift, not necessarily 7–3 if that doesn't work for the classroom. While employee needs outside the center must be considered, they must always be within the context of what is best for the program. The center is in much better shape if employees understand the fundamental purpose of the center is to support the families needing care. Staff hours are determined by those needs. There are other ways to accommodate staff needs.

■ **Know how staff relates to each other.** It is important to have a healthy dynamic between the adults working together. It is not necessary for staff to be best friends or to even be friends outside the center, but they must be able to maintain a professional relationship with the other people on their team. It is important to facilitate, encourage, and expect staff to work out the personal issues that may come up. A staff change is not automatic if people don't want to work together anymore. However, there are times when a change has to be

---

Appendix A

The attachments include a sheet with examples of staff scheduling patterns and a sheet with the budget needed to use those patterns.

Some notes:

The staffing patterns are each a little different. Take note of the planning and break times included in the day. B = break and P = planning time.

Example 1 — The lead teacher and teacher work an 8-hour shift with a half-hour planning time and half-hour break. The assistant teachers both work a 4-hour shift with no planning or break time.

Example 2 — The lead teacher and teacher work an 8-hour shift with a half-hour planning time and a half-hour break. The assistant teachers work a 5-hour shift with a half-hour planning time and a half-hour break.

Example 3 — The lead teacher and teacher work an 8.5-hour shift with a 1-hour break (a half-hour is unpaid) and a half-hour planning time. The assistant teachers work a 5-hour shift with a half-hour planning time and a half-hour break (all paid).

Example 4 — The lead teacher and teacher work an 8.5-hour shift with a 1-hour break (a half-hour unpaid) and a half-hour planning time. One assistant teacher works a 5-hour shift and the other a 5.5-hour shift with a half-hour planning time and a half-hour break (all paid). In example 4, all staff would only be able to leave if there were substitutes available. Otherwise, two could go together while the other two remained with the children.

Years 2 and 3 assume a 7% pay increase each year and no turnover. A 7% pay increase is more than what you would typically see in a child care program. It is also not typical for a center to experience no turnover in any of the groups, so the costs for years 2 and 3 are inflated from what will be the likely reality.

Take note of the differences in costs compared to the schedules. There is a small difference in cost for a noticeable and dramatic difference in coverage.

© Lori Harris 11/1/03

Appendix B — Group Count Form

The times are inserted for a program open from 6 a.m. to 7 p.m. Monday – Friday

Time	Monday	Tuesday	Wednesday	Thursday	Friday
6:00					
6:15					
6:30					
6:45					
7:00					
7:15					
7:30					
8:00					
8:30					
9:00					
9:30					
10:00					
11:00					
12:00					
12:30					
1:00					
2:00					
3:00					
4:00					
4:30					
5:00					
5:30					
5:45					
6:00					
6:15					
6:30					
6:45					
7:00					

made. A teacher may leave to have a baby and a teacher aide may be promoted into the position from another room, leaving a hole to fill with someone new. Staff transitions — even when they are within the center — can be very difficult for some children and families. It is important to be able to articulate why the change is happening for anyone who wants to know.

■ **Ask two questions.** When all is said and done, directors should ask themselves the following two questions:

- If I were working this shift could my professional needs be met? Would it be okay for me?

- If my child was in this classroom, could her or his needs be met with this staffing pattern? Would it be okay for her or him?

The time and attention we spend on staff is enormous, and scheduling is just one of the tasks involved. The schedule does affect the emotional state of the people who work the shifts. Attention to the needs of the adults as well as the children is key. And you'll know what to say when that great candidate asks that not-so-dreaded-anymore question at the end of the interview.

Final Thoughts

Scheduling people is not easy. There are many perspectives to consider. Understand that it won't work out perfectly every time and that your best laid plans could go completely awry. However, if time is spent gathering basic information and implementing a staff schedule that takes this basic information into account, the ongoing time spent in scheduling is minimized. And if staff understands that the schedules and needs of the families and children are what ultimately determine the center's operation, partnerships form between staff and families that can only enrich a child's life.

Lori Harris

Lori Harris is the Executive Director for the Children's Center of the Upper Valley in Lebanon, New Hampshire. She is also the owner of the Center for Learning, Adventure and Discovery, LLC, a developing outdoor classroom and training environment. She teaches Financial Management for the Champlain College Early Childhood Graduate program and for the Connecticut Credentialing system through CT Charts a Course. She is a proud member of the new Exceptional Master Leader group. Lori taught for Wheelock College in Singapore during January and February 2016.

3 CHAPTER 3
Raising Funds to Support Quality

Secrets of Successful Fundraisers

by Dawn Marie Barhyte

It's no secret that child care programs need more financial help today than ever before. A well-planned and enjoyable fundraising campaign can make all the difference in raising the monies needed to supplement stretched budgets.

With all the options available today, you may have difficulty choosing a fundraising strategy. Start by asking yourself what you hope to accomplish. Are you looking to raise fast monies or do you want an event that will get families and the community involved? A simple desire to raise funds does not guarantee success. Successful fundraisers require strategic thinking, careful planning, organization, and commitment. When plotting your course, there are some fundraising fundamentals to consider that can really boost profits.

Begin by assessing your readiness. With dedication and meticulous planning, your fundraising efforts can be a resounding success. A written fundraising plan gives you a road map for achieving your goals. Having a clear focus and well-organized plan keeps enthusiasm and commitment high, which will maximize results. Listed are tips on how to get started securing your share of the millions raised every day:

■ **Set smart goals for the fundraiser.** Marc Pitman, author of *Ask without Fear* and a fund-raising coach, says, "Most folks have no idea how much they want to raise. You can't hit a target if you don't set one." Setting smart goals is a critical step in the fundraising process because it gives supporters confidence to support your organization through their donations and it gives your team the confidence they need to work towards that goal. SMART goals are:

- **S**pecific
- **M**easurable
- **A**ttainable
- **R**elevant
- **T**imely

Specific, achievable goals give supporters something concrete to put money behind. This will allow you to evaluate products, events, and programs that are ideal for your center.

■ **Communicate your fundraising goals.** Your audience should include prospective supporters; your message should include the benefits to the community. The more clearly you state your goal, the more easily you can convince supporters of your fundraising campaign's worthiness. To create a buzz, Little Angels held a fundraiser kickoff party with donated refreshments for their staff and parents to communicate their fundraising goal of raising $5,000 and the benefits to the community, followed by a plea to the community in their local papers and on the local radio station.

> Little Angels Child Care needs to raise money to purchase classroom computers. They set a goal of $5,000 plus $500 they will need to spend on advertising to get there. That total is their fundraising goal. (i.e., desired profit – expenses = fundraising goal). A local corporation matched the $2,500 they raised in raffle tickets, doubling their efforts. They purchased computers with the funds, making their child care program more desirable to area families.

- **Decide what you hope to accomplish in the next year.** All My Children Day Care staff evaluated their program and concluded that they need to update their office technology in order to better serve the families who rely on them to care for their children.

- **Articulate your organization's main objectives and target audience.** Identify not only what you do, but also the difference you make in the lives of the families you serve. Experts say one of the biggest pitfalls of fundraising is that programs don't know their communities. For example, St. Bernard's Head Start held a pancake breakfast to raise funds so they can purchase developmentally-appropriate books for their lending library. This strategy is appropriate for their audience. They raised enough money to purchase a wonderful selection of multicultural books that families can enjoy together and boost literacy. Had they decided on an upscale event to raise monies, they would have been unsuccessful.

- **Tell your unique story and show your passion for your cause.** People want to know what they are being asked to support, why it's important to donate now, where their donations will go, and that they will have a positive impact. One key

> All My Children Day Care decided to host a children's sing-along. They hired a children's performer, pre-sold tickets, scheduled the event for a weekend afternoon, and sold child-friendly snacks. This child-centered event honored their mission: All My Children Day Care provides a supportive, fun, and safe home-away-from-home for the children in their care. We seek community support to further our mission.

to successful fundraising is knowing why you are doing it in the first place. Raise community awareness of what you need, how the public can help, and what you offer in return. People who can identify with a cause are more likely to be generous. Joe Garecht, author of *How to Raise Money for Any Non-profit*, says, "People need to identify with the problem that the non-profit is trying to solve, be moved by the problem, and be convinced that the non-profit is providing the correct solution to solve or alleviate the problem." Make it easy for supporters and families by telling them exactly where the money will go and what their support enables your organization to do. To capture the hearts of supporters, make your case interesting and appealing to affect the community personally.

> All My Children Day Care did this in one sentence; telling their story in an emotionally engaging and easy-to-deliver pitch: *All My Children Day Care provides an affordable, loving, educational environment that promotes the needs of the whole child and his or her family.*

- **Choose the right fundraiser.** If the perfect idea is backed up by a well-organized plan, your fundraiser can be a huge success.

- **Create a plan.** Every fundraising event needs a plan. According to Joe Garecht of the Fundraising

Union Child Care started strategizing early by conducting research on what other local organizations had done recently to raise funds. They knew if they duplicated these efforts they would be unsuccessful. Understanding that the fundraising strategy should be a good match to the mission and purpose of its organization, they chose a carnival. This met the community need for budget-friendly family fun events. Money raised from the event was used to develop a new playground.

Authority, "Events take time and money — scarce resources for non-profits. You need to ensure it's worth it to hold the event." Here's one example of a multi-step fundraising plan.

■ **Select the event or product that fits your prospective supporters.** There is a lot of competition for people's time and money. To ensure your

First, Union carefully evaluated its fundraising goals to ensure the activity was worth the effort. Again, they asked themselves what they were hoping to accomplish. Although a huge effort was needed for a relatively small payoff, they would raise community awareness of their services so this was a huge plus. They worked up a realistic budget, keeping costs low by relying on donations wherever possible. (Many local businesses were willing to donate, as long as they were mentioned as supporters.) Later in the year, Union created festive holiday baskets of goodies donated by local merchants that were raffled off. Still later, they created and sold coupon books with deals from local businesses and solicited sponsors such as local restaurants. Supporters were recognized at the campaign launch and in the center newsletter.

fundraising efforts are successful, ask yourself the following questions:

- Why will people want to attend our event?

- What is unique about it?

- What will happen as a result of their short- and long-term support?

The type of product or event that 'sells' best is the one that appeals most to your audience or supporters. Think of potential supporters as consumers: Is this something they already use or does the event appeal to them?

Union targeted young families for their carnival event. They organized child-friendly games and booths that cost a nominal fee: face painting, slime for sensory play, sand art, and ring toss. The real benefits were apparent only after the event concluded. The event attracted new enrollment, while raising the $3,000 that was necessary to upgrade the playground.

■ **Keep it simple and consider repeat events.** Don't be afraid of doing what has worked before. For example, bake sales are usually a big hit and can be very profitable because most families will not hesitate to donate or purchase homemade goodies.

Experts recommend that you size up product fundraisers with a little research; these are usually easy to distribute and profits are high. Your cost depends on the product you choose and how many cases you purchase. When choosing a product fundraiser, be sure to inquire how long they have been in business, how much initial costs are, and the company's reputation. Those companies with high-quality products, a good track record, and who are easy to work with are more likely to boost your bottom line.

> With a nod to the diversity in their community, Warwick Child Care asked staff and families to bake something that reflects their heritage for its annual sale. To get to its fundraising goal faster, Warwick Child Care brings in a supplementary product fundraiser (greeting cards and wrapping paper) to boost profits.

Thank donors. Marc Pitman, the Fundraising Coach says,

> "One of the worst things you can do is ask for money, then ask again and again. A good rule of thumb is to thank people between asks." He adds, "Share news in terms of gratitude for those who have given to your cause or attended special fundraising events. People love thanks in all sorts of ways. Some like a public display, while others much prefer a handwritten note. Although this is time-consuming, people are worth it!"

Conclusion

Fundraising may seem daunting at first, but if you keep the basics in mind you may find that you not only raise money for your child care center, build community awareness of your services, make friends, but have fun doing it! There are many ways to fundraise and while there is no fool-proof formula, there are fundamentals that can really make a difference and allow you to confidently raise the monies your organization needs to grow. Fundraising can be a vital part of your annual budgeting, creating a stronger and more financially secure organization.

According to Joe Garecht, the most successful fundraising team leaders share three qualities:

1) They are not afraid to lead, they believe in the mission of their organization, and are willing to forge a strategy to further the needs of the organization.

2) They know how to get the job done.

3) They are the hardest working.

Fundraising is a collaborative effort, so get everyone involved: staff, families, local merchants, corporations, and the community. Work together towards your program's long-term success.

References

Garecht, J. (n.d.). "How to raise money for any non-profit." Available: www.thefundraisingauthority.com

Pitman, M. A. (2007). *Ask without fear*. Mechanicsburg, PA: Executive Books.

Dawn Marie Barhyte

Dawn Marie Barhyte is a freelance author who has been published widely. She writes frequently on early childhood topics, child development, and parenting issues. For over 20 years she met the needs of children and their families co-directing, teaching, and coordinating children's programs. She continues her commitment to children and touches their lives through her writing.

Fundraising Success Stories

by Roger Neugebauer

Exchange invited readers to share their fundraising success stories and received a wide variety of innovative responses.

Summer Sips and Strokes

Our event was a Paint and Wine Party with silent auction. We hired a paint and sip studio artist to provide instructions to attendees about painting while tasting different wines provided by One Hope Wines. We cleared more than $3,600 for our first fundraiser. Organizing points:

■ Be strategic about the size; sometimes small is best. We sold out at 48 people.

■ Silent auction — plan ahead. MANY big corporations plan to give away items for auctions, but you need to allow at least 6 to 8 weeks to apply.

■ Events give people an opportunity to donate instead of attending. Even if you know people can't attend, invite them and give them a link to donate 'in lieu of attending.'

Samantha Marshall
Moorpark, California

Art Auction

Each fall the teachers save the children's artwork. We put a number on each piece and display it outside the classrooms for a week. We put auction bid slips in various places as well as boxes for the slips; we raise about $500 with no cost to us, since the children would be creating art anyway. The pieces go to the highest bidder. We correlate it with our lunch buddies, where each child invites someone to have lunch with them, so we have more grandparents visiting as well as aunts and uncles, instead of just parents.

Diane Hendrick
Youngwood, Pennsylvania

Fish Wish Annual Fundraising Campaign

Three years ago, we switched from a fundraising model centered on an annual auction to a direct-ask fundraising campaign that encourages parents to identify what they value about the education their child receives at our school, and to share this with other parents, extended family members, friends, and through their community connections. Parents are invited to couple this storytelling with a request for individuals to join them in supporting the school with a financial contribution. Last year we raised $90,000, with 91% of families making a contribution, and we decreased our fundraising overhead from 30% to 4%. By utilizing a volunteer team of parents, board members, and educators, we freed up administrative resources, while simultaneously enlisting powerful fundraising supporters.

Joel Metschke
Seattle, Washington

Karm'l Apple Fundraiser

Every October around Halloween, the center (parents and staff) sell caramel apples to fundraise for a particular goal, such as paying for a field trip. We make an average of $1,000. Organizing points:

- Send out all fundraising information and material at the beginning of the month.

- Be clear on the goal and how that is going to benefit their child

- Send a weekly reminder, and be enthusiastic about it!

Yeni Portillo
Los Angeles, California

Tree of Giving

We seek to instill and nurture the concept of giving back. First, create a cohesive feeling for the Graduating Class each year. The Graduating Class of children and their parents gives a Thank You 'gift' to the Center (i.e., a piece of equipment, books, a painting project, or similar gesture). Thereafter, each Class is asked to support and give dollars to the year's Graduating Class based on their own financial capacity. It means maintaining a database of families and children with a request each spring to 'give' back. Even if only 10% respond, it's more than 0%. A sense

of continuity and community develops. This works when there are positive relationships with families and the leadership is invested in maintaining a long-term focus as an excellent ECE community.

Luis Hernandez
Miami, Florida

Art Afaire

Our event is an annual silent auction and raffle that is held at an art gallery owned by parents of children at our school. We solicit many local businesses to acquire donations, and auction and raffle items such as Disneyland tickets, stays at hotels, gym memberships, and even a guitar signed by a famous musician. But, the most sought-after items we auction are one-of-a-kind pieces of art created by our preschoolers. The children work together to create beautiful masterpieces on canvas that are the highlight of the event. The fundraiser is always a success and the funds are used for our staff development.

Debbie Midcalf
Palm Desert, California

Quilt Raffle

Our biggest fundraiser during the 30+ years I was on the Board of a small center serving children of low-income means was when one of our Board members donated a handmade quilt and we raffled that off. We sold more raffle tickets for that quilt than we ever did for candy or chocolate gift boxes or for plants and flowers. We made nearly $500. People seemed to love the idea of winning and owning a handmade quilt.

Alice Honig
Syracuse, New York

Rethinking Fundraising

In our multi-site child care agency, we used to do 14 different fundraisers: golf tournaments, chocolate bar sales, poinsettia sales, spirit wear, and much more. Chocolate bar sales were the most profitable. We'd raise about $15,000 per year. However, as time went on, people were becoming tired of selling. We then gave families the option to make a donation in lieu of selling chocolate bars and provided a suggested donation of $35 (what we earned per case of chocolate bars). This proved very successful. That being said, in 2012, our Board decided to no longer do active fundraising. Research showed that our fundraisers targeted the parents of the children we serve and they were already paying high child care fees.

Lori Prospero
Kitchener, Ontario

Annual Silent Auction and Gala

We do only one fundraiser every year: our annual Silent Auction and Gala, an adult only semi-formal event. The parents form an auction committee and work as a team to solicit donations from the community, scout sites for the event, organize food and drinks, and set up. The teachers make classroom projects to auction off. The event was held at the large home of one of the grandparents, who underwrote some of the expenses. In the three years we held the event we raised $17,000, then $21,000, then $27,000 (before expenses)! The key was having a parent group that worked well together, met regularly over wine and food, and had their own celebration afterwards for a job well done.

Florie Reber
Tampa, Florida

United Way Community Building Grant

Nabor House Community applied for the United Way Community Building Grant and was awarded $9,088 to implement parent programming that will be focused on SLAM (Science, Literacy, Art, and Math). This grant will provide for quarterly parent events and take-home science kits that include a children's book. With the current early childhood focus, there are grants available to strengthen programs. Research, including looking at funders of similar organizations and grant searches, are the starting point.

Barbara Allen
Houston, Texas

Read-a-thon

Each child recruited sponsors for the total amount of books they could read, or had read to them, in two weeks' time. Sponsors chose a dollar amount for each book or flat donation in support. With eight children participating, we raised over $500 — all profit! Average books read per student was 95! One of my students, who is autistic, learned to read during this two-week period! Awesome bonus!

Patti Robinson
Wilmot, Wisconsin

Art's Nite

We held a fundraiser where we showcased and sold children's artwork. At the fundraiser we discussed in-depth children's collaborative process, highlighting the mediums used. We discussed what children gained from these experiences. Giving parents a clear understanding of the high-quality curriculum, parents were eager to bid on the stunning 20" x 40" framed pieces. There were limited pieces so a 'bidding war' began and drove the prices up.

The fundraiser brought in over $2,500 for a small preschool. Our success was due to children working collaboratively on large paper, using quality artist materials, and framing the work. We provided meaning to the pieces by discussing them, and provided parents with a list of materials that would be bought with the money raised.

Suraiya Daud
La Crescenta, California

Crab Feed

We have an annual Crab Feed each winter. It is the ONE fundraiser we do and each parent MUST purchase two tickets. A strong core team is a MUST! Co-chair, silent auction, raffle, dessert raffle, class raffles, decorations, tickets. We have made profits of $16,000 (during our lowest year) up to $26,000 (net).

Tammy Hamilton-Williams
Stockton, California

Purse Bingo

Participants play Bingo, and the prizes are designer purses. During the event, participants play nine cards per game with a total of 15 games. In 2014, the event netted $7,000. Key points:

- Recruit as many sponsors as possible. Ask for donations of money instead of purses, because styles change so frequently.

- You will need an experienced Bingo caller, volunteers, and a strong committee.

- Create a plan for double and triple Bingo winners for each game. If you have 15 games, you will need approximately 45 purses.

- Anticipate that you will need to supply Bingo dobbers, define how to win each game (Bingo participants are serious), small snacks and beverages. We like to give participants swag bags that have everything included.

Amy Richardson
Sewickley, Pennsylvania

Fall HoeDown

Our parent board put on our first Fall Fundraiser in October 2014. We sold tickets to families and church members. We gathered free items for a silent auction, a band played for free, a local dance studio taught line dancing, we sold pieces of pizza at $1 a slice (donated from a local pizza parlor), a photographer set up a booth and took family photos, a face painter donated her time and the children lined up to have their faces painted. We set up our indoor climber for the children to play on — supervised by their parents. We charged $25/family to attend from 6-8 pm. We brought in over $3,000. Our theme this year is Under the Big Top.

Barb Wigstadt
Bloomington, Minnesota

Roger Neugebauer

Roger Neugebauer is founding publisher of *Exchange Magazine* and a co-founder of the World Forum Foundation.

Securing Funds through Grant Writing

by Fredalene Bowers

Funding is always a concern for child care centers. It doesn't matter whether the program is non-profit or for-profit, privately owned or corporate-sponsored, large or small, there never seems to be enough money to cover personnel expenses and purchase equipment and materials. Most child care directors depend on federal or state allocations, parent fees, and fundraising to meet financial needs. The idea of securing additional funds through grant writing is often not a consideration because the process seems overwhelming, and often the director is not aware of grants as a source of additional funding. If your program is seeking additional funding, grant writing might be your answer. This article will address two aspects to securing funds through grant writing: first, how to apply for grants and second, where to apply.

Understanding the Grant Writing Process

Grant writing is not as difficult as many people believe. Although there are courses on grant writing, very few people start their career with the goal of "becoming a grant writer." Most individuals become grant writers out of necessity — they need to maintain their current funding, they need to secure additional funding to supplement current funds,

and/or they want to introduce new programs. The following are some tried and true tips to help the beginning grant writer.

Top 10 Tips:

10 — Assess your chances for success

It is best to start small where competition is not so stiff. Before you begin to tackle the proposal, find out how much money is available and how many grants will be funded. It will be easier to secure a local or state grant for 5-, 10-, or 20-thousand dollars than a federal grant where millions of dollars are available but only 15 proposals will be funded.

9 — Get to know your funder

Funders have a reason for funding projects. No matter how great you think your idea is or how much your program will benefit by the funding, if your goals do not match the funder's goals, you are wasting your time by applying. Many federal, state, and private funders have a "Pre-Proposal Conference" or "Bidders Conference" to identify the purpose of the funding, the amount of funding, the number of grants to be awarded, and guidelines for submitting the proposal. If possible, attend these in person. You may be able to meet the funders or their representatives. If you can't attend, many funders will mail, within ten days to two weeks, the questions and answers addressed at the conference. Knowing your funder is important. Your success rate increases 300%, if you know your funder (CD Publications, 193-94).

8 — Set up a proposal library

There are many commonalities when writing a proposal. All proposals require information about your organization: the history, mission statement, staffing patterns (organizational chart), job descriptions, number of children served, ability to carry out the proposal, current staff résumés, and program demographics. This information is called 'boilerplate material.' Start files for boilerplate material and continually add items (e.g. current statistics) so the material is at your fingertips when you need it.

7 — Follow the directions exactly and pay attention to details

Grant writing is not a creative activity. The funder is looking for an innovative project, not innovative or creative writing; therefore, it is essential that you follow the directions exactly. Most proposal formats are similar; an abstract or summary (if proposal is over ten pages), a table of contents, a problem or need statement, goals and objectives, target population, project methodology/work plan, organizational capability, evaluation, budget, and appendix/attachments. Read and reread the directions, then follow them: number of pages, headings, size of margins, format. It is also extremely important to pay attention to the deadline. If the proposal is due by 4:00 pm on September 30, allow enough time for delivery by mail or plan to hand deliver it, if this is acceptable to the funder.

Read the guidelines carefully so you know how the funds are to be used (and how they cannot be used). Many small grants cannot be used to purchase equipment. So no matter how badly your program needs a new computer or copier, don't write those into the budget. When I asked participants at a recent grant writing workshop to brainstorm innovative projects to fund, one participant responded "… textbooks because our school does not have up-to-date textbooks." As I told the group, most funders will not provide money for textbooks since this is the responsibility of the school. However, if the proposal is for a course using innovative techniques and strategies, you may be able to purchase textbooks with some of the grant monies.

Methodology or Work Plan

Be very specific in writing your methodology section. This is where grant writing often falls short. You may know what you want to do but your funder does not, so include all of the relevant details. State exactly how, when, what, and who will be involved. Use the narrative format to explain your proposal. It is better to include more details here than less. Remember, the reviewer/funder has no idea what you are thinking, so be specific. Include your goals and objectives separately. Most funders want the objectives written in measurable, behavioral terms such as 'to increase,' 'to improve,' or 'to expand.' Avoid objectives that begin 'to understand,' which cannot be measured and are not behavioral objectives.

The goals and objectives can be identified in a timeline or PERT (Program Evaluation and Review Technique) Chart. This format includes the goals and objectives on the left, the responsible party (to carry out the goals/objectives listed next), then a timeline with the expected completion date identified.

6 — Emphasize experience and qualifications

This is your opportunity to 'toot your own horn.' Briefly discuss your history in the field: "Our program has over ten years of experience in the field of child care and maintains a reputation for providing high-quality, developmentally appropriate programming." You might also address the educational level of the director and teachers. If your program has completed an evaluation or parent survey, discuss the positive aspects of the evaluation/survey.

If possible, use the appendix/attachments to include newspaper clippings of your program, support letters from parents/families, and photographs of relevant activities.

5 — Seek support from local and state politicians

This is when politicians become your best friends, especially if you are seeking local or state funding. Contact your legislator's aides to discuss ways to fund your idea or project. The function of legislative aides is to help the constituents — that's you! Ask your state representatives about discretionary funds (once called "WAMs" or "Walking Around Money") used to support programs or projects in their area. These are small pots of money, but it might be just what you need to begin a new project.

Don't be shy about inviting local and state representatives to visit your program. If you do receive funding, send photos to your legislators, or better yet, invite the legislator to visit your program, along with a photographer from the local newspaper. Legislators love to have their pictures taken with worthwhile community projects. Market your program and activities so your political leaders and your community understand and support your program.

4 — Use current statistics and data

Support your request for funds with statistics. Use statistics from newspapers or journals to support your proposal. Local agencies are also good sources of statistics:

Contact the job center/employment center; departments of public welfare, health, education, and/or labor and industry; extension office; county courthouse or human services office; school

districts for additional information. The Internet is a wonderful tool for grant writing, with statistics at your fingertips. Use search engines for information on children and families. Current national statistics on children and families can be obtained from the Children's Defense Fund (www.childrensdefense.org). When using statistics and data, compare your program with local, state, and/or national statistics to make a case for funding.

3 — Collaborate and cooperate

These are sometimes referred to as "The Big C's" for funding. Funders want to stretch the dollars as far as possible, and the best way to do this is for agencies/programs to work together. There are many benefits to collaboration — more innovative ideas, more individuals willing to provide support letters, sharing resources, and providing in-kind match. In-kind match is often required and may be either cash or support services and goods. Cash match is actual dollars, which is often difficult because most agencies are financially strapped. Support services and goods are defined as individual volunteer service and donations of office space or supplies. I have provided in-kind services for grants as a volunteer child development consultant, at the rate of $100 per hour for 20 hours (July 1–June 30), thus an in-kind match of $2,000. You may find financial experts, business executives, and secretaries willing to volunteer their time as a match.

Include on your advisory board some movers and shakers. These are individuals who may have connections for funds, individuals who have expertise in grant writing, and/or individuals who can serve as consultants for your program and for your proposal.

2 — Proofread and recalculate

This is essential. The proposal is your sales pitch — it says "Pick Me." It is extremely important to proofread, especially if you have more than one writer. The writers may have very different styles, so one individual needs to be responsible for the final copy. Also, have a staff member read the final proposal. By the time you get to your final copy, you have read and rewritten the proposal so often that you read over the errors.

Budgets

It is important to work with a fiscal person to ensure that your figures and calculations are correct. I reviewed one proposal where no personnel benefits were included. That program would have been very surprised if they had received the requested amount, only to find out they couldn't offer the anticipated salaries because the grant was $10,000 short in monies to pay benefits.

1 — Learn from rejection

If the funder did not love your proposal as much as you had hoped and fails to fund it, do not be discouraged. Contact the funder and request a critique or debriefing about why your proposal was not successful. (Sometimes funders will meet with the unsuccessful applicants individually.) Using their feedback, rewrite your proposal and resubmit for the next funding cycle or seek another funding source. Always save your proposals; they can often be recycled. Remember, the funder wants to give away the money as long as your proposal matches their goals, objectives, and requirements.

Where to Look for Grants — Start Locally

We have all heard the phrase "Success breeds success." Therefore, in order to be successful at grant writing, the best way is to begin small. Look for local or state grants.

On the local level, many social service organizations fund community-based projects; check your local Kiwanis, Rotary Club, Jaycees, Lions Clubs, and others. Women's organizations such as the Zonta

Club, American Association of University Women, and Junior Women's Civic Club may also fund projects. Some counties have Human Services Development Programs, which allocate small sums to community organizations. Local businesses may provide funds for community projects through mini-grants; contact retail stores such as Walmart, banks, and grocery stores.

The State Level

On the state level, use the Internet to locate information on grants from the departments of public welfare, health, education and/or labor and industry. If you can't find information this way or you don't have access to the Internet, try calling the department directly and talk with personnel to garner information about locating funding sources.

State and National Foundations

State and national foundations are an excellent source of grant monies; however, they are often harder to obtain since they are more competitive. The best way to find funding sources to match your purpose, your interests, and/or your geographic region is through the 'Foundation Center.' This is an independent national service organization that provides an overview of private funding foundations. Information about the center can be accessed at www.fdncenter.org. Another source for funding opportunities is CD Publications (www.cdpublications.com). This is an excellent publication (although fairly expensive, $369 per year) with newsletters covering everything from housing to education. Check out the Children & Youth Funding Report Newsletter. This report publishes 24 issues per year and covers grants, foundations, research, and reports in the field. A free, 14–18 page sample newsletter can be accessed from their site.

Federal Funds

The "Federal Register" is the grandfather of all federal grants. This publication provides notices of funding availability (NOFA) issued by all agencies of the federal government, and all regulations and guidelines. Although expert grant writers use this publication regularly, novices may find it a bit overwhelming. The cost of a subscription is expensive, over $300 per year; however, many libraries carry subscriptions.

These are just a few suggestions to get you started as a grant writer and to paraphrase Dr. Seuss (1990), "Today is your day. You're off to Great Proposals! You're off and away!"

References

Bauer, D. G. (1994). *Grantseeking primer for classroom leaders.* New York: Scholastic.

CD Publications. (1993-94, Winter). "Federal Assistance Monitor Grant Update Bulletin" [Brochure]. Silver Spring, MD.

CD Publications. "Children & youth funding report." [Online] Retrieved July 19, 2004: www.cdpublications.com.

Ferguson, J. (1992). *The grantseeker's guide to project evaluation.* Alexandria, VA: Capitol Publications Inc.

Government Information Services. (1993). *111 secrets to smarter grantsmanship.* Arlington, VA.

Seuss, D. (1990). *Oh, the places you'll go.* New York: Random House.

Fredalene Bowers

Fredalene B. Bowers, Ph.D., a former preschool teacher and center director, is an Associate Professor of Child Development and Family Relations at Indiana University of Pennsylvania, in Indiana, Pennsylvania. She was also a grant writer and program coordinator for at-risk children and families and grant reviewer for state and local grants. She presents state and national workshops on grant writing and a variety of child development topics.

Fishing for Dollars in Philanthropic Waters

by Anne Mitchell

Every child care director, at some point, has confronted the fact that parents (even well-off ones) just can't pay enough to support good child care services. The savvy director is always looking for new sources of funding and evaluating whether they're worth pursuing. If we could become a United Way agency, would the effort be worth it? What could we do as a fundraiser besides another bake sale? Is buying lottery tickets a good investment? Somewhere in this process, the idea of soliciting foundations comes up. Probably right after you hear that some national child care group just got a multi-million dollar grant from You-Name-It foundation, you think: Why couldn't we do that? This article is for you.

First, let's be clear that foundations are not now (or ever) going to be the direct source of funding that solves the compensation-affordability problem. Foundations are not and never will be the main source of funding for any child care center's operation. The direct services or general operating expenses of any organization are almost never supported by philanthropy. The role that foundations play in a field is something like what an entrepreneur does improve, expand, and innovate. The difference is that foundations do this indirectly through the work of those organizations they fund, rather than directly as an entrepreneur would in operating a business.

Foundations are looking for innovative solutions to problems, promising approaches to improve on current methods, or expansions of successful programs that address a problem. Expanding services for families (adding or starting new programs), improving practice through professional development, linking child care services with other services families need are all examples of child care ideas foundations might consider supporting.

Foundations correctly believe their role in child care is to help the field solve problems and address current needs, not to become a direct funder of services. Given that cautionary note, foundations can and will fund child care if you approach the right ones in the right way.

The Philanthropic Landscape

Philanthropy comes in many forms, from individual donors to national foundations. This article focuses on philanthropic entities (foundations and corporations) that might support local child care projects. If you want to know how to find major individual donors, that's another story (actually, a set of unique and non-replicable stories). Understanding something about the types of foundations and their basic characteristics can help you identify the right ones to consider pursuing.

All foundations are legal entities designed to give away money for particular purposes to other non-profit entities. Many were established with the funds from one individual, one family (or extended family), or one corporation. Others are collections of funds bequeathed by many different individuals and families. Some foundations are restricted to support-ing certain types of work or particular geographic areas either by the will of those who gave the money or the wishes of the current trustees.

Foundations can have a national, regional, and/or local focus in their grant making. Some national foundations also have a local grant-making program to benefit the community they reside in. Commu-nity foundations are usually collections of trusts and bequests that are restricted to a specific community. Community foundations often have the word 'com-munity' or 'area' in their names, e.g. the Rochester Area Foundation or the Marin Community Founda-tion.

Corporate foundations (or a corporation's annual charitable giving) focus mainly (or solely) on those communities where the corporation has worksites and employees. Community foundations and cor-porate foundations with a local focus are probably the most likely to support local child care projects. National foundations with a diverse local grants program may also be supporters.

Foundations can legally only give money to certain types of organizations almost always a not-for-profit corporation, which has tax-exempt status [a 501(c)3 organization]. Most non-profit child care centers would qualify, but for-profit centers generally cannot receive funds directly from a foundation. However, associations of providers such as a family child care association or a for-profit directors' association can qualify if the association is incorporated as a non-profit and has tax-exempt status.

Generally, a foundation establishes a set of pro-gram areas, priorities, or strategies that guide its grant making. Child care is unlikely to be a distinct program priority all by itself, but child care easily fits into a broader area — such as child and youth development, community building, strengthening families, early education and school readiness, or prevention, which are typical philanthropic program areas.

In larger foundations, each program area is the responsibility of an individual program officer. Smaller foundations may have only one staff person who covers all the areas. In some cases, one of the foundation's directors manages the grant making as a volunteer. Knowing whether there is a program area where child care would fit and which foundation staff person handles the area where child care fits are essential pieces of information to have.

Foundations generally make grants based on thoughtful, well-written proposals that directly address the specified issues within a program area. Sending a proposal — no matter how brilliant the ideas in it might be — is not the best way to intro-duce yourself to a foundation. Very few foundations will read and respond to proposals sent 'cold.' Some foundations do not accept unsolicited proposals at all — they will return them unread — because they only fund projects that are developed at their request by organizations they select. Others only accept short letter proposals that follow a specified format. Before you make a move, you must know how each founda-tion approaches grant-making and what its require-ments are for applicants or grant seekers.

What Foundations Fund

Given that foundations will not underwrite your center's parent fees, what will they support? Answer: Improvements and innovations that solve child care problems and benefit the wider community. Profes-sional development is a good example. If the com-munity lacks infant care, a proposal from a group of centers to collectively train their infant care teachers in a manner that would institutionalize an infant care course in the community college might be a fundable proposal. Building the infant care rooms might be fundable if you could find a foundation that supports capital projects, so called 'bricks and mortar.'

Another example is collaborations to expand services. If the community's Head Start grantee and a child care center(s) wanted to jointly provide comprehensive all-day early education, a foundation might fund the planning and start-up phase of such a venture.

Fundraising — no matter whether it is selling raffle tickets or writing a grant proposal — is not begging. You are offering someone an opportunity to support a worthy organization or project and, in the case of a foundation, an opportunity to give away money that the foundation is required by law to give away. Successful fundraising is the combination of four elements:

- a credible, trustworthy person,

- with good ideas for feasible projects,

- that match the foundation's goals, and

- will be carried out in an organization that is financially solid and well managed.

Technically, grant making is the act of one organization making a grant to another organization. Actually, successful grant making is the result of positive human interactions — the foundation officer and the grant seeker establish a working relationship based on good communication and mutual trust that leads eventually to the approval of a grant. Foundations fund people — people they know, people they trust, people with good ideas. Child care center directors who are active in their community are more likely to encounter potential funders in situations where relationships can be established — such as at community meetings or events — than directors who only venture out to attend an occasional conference with their early childhood colleagues.

Getting Started

Many people think the first step is to make a list of all the geographically appropriate foundations that have any history of 'giving to early childhood.' On the contrary, the place to start is with ideas (although research on funders may be needed later). The goal is to make a match between your good ideas and a foundation's goals. Matchmaking is done by people — your ideas will be shaped and changed (improved, hopefully) through your interactions with the foundation officer.

Begin by developing some ideas for projects that would benefit your organization and the wider child care community. This can be done alone, but often goes faster in a small group (if everyone is clear on the task). You might get the local directors' group to brainstorm ideas. After you get a list, pick out the three or four ideas that seem most feasible and write a one-page description of each idea. The 'who, what, where, when, why, how' approach used by newspaper reporters is a good way to start. Write down what the project is, why it is needed, who will do it, how long it will last, what results it will have, and what it will cost.

Because human relationships are important in philanthropic fund raising, another good method for getting started is to think about your own networks and contacts in terms of potential funders. Are any of the people you already know potential funders — that is, connected in some way with corporations or foundations? What about your board — who do they know? Some of your board members may well know philanthropic leaders and be willing to discuss child care with them and introduce you to them directly.

Finally, think about your staff and parents. Some of them may have networks that include potential funders. Don't underestimate your parents. One source of corporate funds for child care is the AT&T Development Fund. A child care provider must be recommended by an AT&T employee to access these funds, which are available for child care improvement and expansion in AT&T communities.

Chances are, if there's a community foundation in your area, you've heard of it. If not, look in the phone book or go to the library. There are a number of published sources of information about foundations that can help you find those in your geographic area that might consider a child care related request.

Your local library may have the current year's Foundation Directory published by the Foundation Center, an information clearinghouse on foundation and corporate giving headquartered in New York City. This directory contains entries for close to 12,000 foundations, giving brief descriptions of their mission and history, total assets, annual grant total, size of an average grant, types of organizations supported, contact information, and any restrictions. The Directory of Corporate Giving has similar entries for over 2,000 corporate grant makers.

If your library does not have these directories, you can contact The Foundation Center directly at (800) 424-9836. They will refer you to the nearest Foundation Center Library or to a Cooperating Collection.

Another way to access information about The Foundation Center is on the Internet: http://fdncenter.org

The process of seeking and receiving foundation funding takes time and effort. Think carefully about whether the process is worth the reward before you start. If it were easy, everyone would be doing it. In fact, some child care center directors have successfully negotiated the foundation waters and are willing to share their lessons.

Anne Mitchell

Anne Mitchell is the president of Early Childhood Policy Research, an independent consulting firm specializing in policy research and planning on child care/early education for government, foundations, and national non-profit organizations. She can be reached at awmitchell@aol.com via the Internet.

Confessions of a Former Funder

by Ann O'Brien

Dear Grantees who I used to fund when I had the checkbook,

I'm sorry. Now that I am in the world of operating a non-profit agency providing early childhood and school-age programs, I'd like to start by saying I'm sorry. While my intentions when I was funding your work were good, I realize better now the impact and burden of some of what I asked of you. I know that our grant applications may have driven you crazy and that the detailed data we requested may have been difficult to gather. I better understand how it feels when funder priorities shift and change. I also realize now that there was probably a cost of doing business with us as your philanthropic partner that I did not fully recognize.

I made the apparently unusual career move of leaving a job where I formerly distributed funds for early childhood and going to one where I am leading an organization that is delivering the services. My new colleagues in the early childhood delivery system don't understand why I would make such a move. I don't understand why I would not. I fell in love with this work while breathing the sometimes rarified air of philanthropy and decided that I wanted to see real parents, children, and teachers every day and not just read about them in grantee reports. That's not to take away from the incredibly important and influ-

ential work that my colleagues in philanthropy do to advance our causes. We could not do this work without them and many continue to be amazing partners. Yet I know now that some may be missing much of the real life, complex, and sometimes seemingly impossible work that happens on the ground every day. We all care about young children, yet manifest that care and concern in so many different ways.

What I have learned in the last two years of living on the front lines is that it's easy to lose sight of the challenges of delivering high-quality services to children and families, what it really costs to do it well, and the need to sustain it over time. I know that when I held the checkbook, I sometimes lost sight of the challenges that my grantees faced and the burdens some of my requirements placed on them. And I'm not sure I always did the best job communicating that reality to my board. Boards in philanthropy need to know that their investments make a difference. That's a real and important demand. But if I knew then what I know now, I might have fought a little harder for you.

The work of philanthropy, like our work, has become much more complicated and much more driven by outcomes and data — as it should be. When you are spending other people's money and trying to change people's lives, different rules apply. My advice to my philanthropic colleagues would be to get out into the field as often as you can and to develop relationships with grantees that are authentic. They need a safe space where they can honestly share failures and challenges. Do what you can to streamline your grant making and reporting systems. And perhaps most importantly, continue to recognize the deep commitment and expertise that resides in your grantees.

I encourage all of us to be bold and brave and to develop careers that shift between sectors in the interest in advancing our shared goals and objectives and developing our own selves as professionals and advocates. We are partners in this work and need to understand each other's perspectives and points of view. We have so much to learn from one another. And when we do that, the real winners are the children and families we serve. And those are the people who brought us to these jobs in the first place.

Ann O'Brien

Ann O'Brien is currently the Chief Executive Officer of Montgomery Early Learning Centers (MELC). Since assuming this position in 2014, Ann has focused on ensuring that all of MELC's early childhood and school-age programs meet the highest standards of quality and expanding access to them. Ann was a collaborator in the Early Childhood Education Workforce Transformation Initiative, which studied the current challenges of the Philadelphia ECE workforce and proposed solutions for improvement. She also serves on the boards of directors of the Early Care and Education Consortium, the Pennsylvania Childcare Association, and Graduate! Philadelphia.

Fundraising for Your Center

An Opportunity to Build Community

by Vicky Tsakoyias-Mendes

People say, "It takes a village to raise a child." In orchestrating a fundraiser for my center, I realized it takes a village to run a successful fundraising event!

Throughout my teaching and directing career, I have enjoyed the planning and implementation of various fundraising events (e.g. t-shirt sales, flower pots, clay ornaments decorated by our children, and bake sales). These types of fundraising events were based on products that were fun, safe, and easy to make, market, and sell. The overhead was low, but so were the returns; the funds generated by these events were just enough to cover a few teachers' training registration fees or to celebrate staff birthdays.

Recently, however, something unexpected happened that pushed my 'creative fundraising' button. Last summer while I was out on maternity leave, the Children's Center Evening Program came close to being shut down due to lack of funding. Following many discussions with the college's president, parents and staff advocated and the evening program, which operates from 5:00 pm–10:00 pm remained open. Meanwhile, a father in our evening program, who is a dance choreographer, offered to dance in order to raise money for the center.

Planning a Fundraiser

On Wednesday, March 25, 2009, the Chabot College Children's Center, located in Hayward, California, hosted their first fundraising venture called "International Arts Performance Recital" at the Chabot College's Theater. This event was a 'cultural journey' traveling virtually around the world in two hours through dance and music. The event's logo was designed to include a world globe signifying our attempt to reach beyond human boundaries and geographical borders.

In planning the fundraiser, we followed these steps:

■ Arranged a meeting with the Chabot Theater manager and theater coordinator to discuss our fundraising idea, as well as cost, availability of the theater for the date we had in mind, and resources for marketing and recruiting performers.

■ Emails were sent to college staff and faculty, local churches, and dance studios recruiting volunteer performers for our multicultural dance event.

■ Flyers were distributed to center parents, staff, Early Childhood Development faculty, and students recruiting volunteer performers and committee members (e.g. marketing, selling tickets, and backstage support).

■ One of our teachers, who is an artist, designed the event's logo and then worked with the college's art designer to create a computer image that was used for event flyers, posters, tickets, VIP invitations, certificates, and thank-you notes.

■ A father-mother team volunteered to emcee the event, the script was written, and a rehearsal took place.

■ Emails were sent to local colleges, center parents, and local business owners about placing a tax-deductible business advertisement of their product or service in our event program.

■ The college's art department created the event program including advertisements.

■ The marketing committee conducted targeted outreach to local ECE agencies (e.g. Head Start, 4 C's, Every Child Counts, Bananas, Alameda County Planning Council, and local elementary schools) in advertising the event. In addition, the event was advertised through the college's electronic sign-board, website, local newspaper, and radio stations.

■ The theater coordinator conducted a tour, reviewing the different acts, multiple stages, curtains, lights, sound, screen availability, balloon-drop equipment, availability of theater crew, VIP seating, and backstage environment.

■ Performers kept in touch with one another through emails and phone calls, keeping everyone up-to-date on details regarding the rehearsal and event schedule.

■ A meeting with the college's security staff clarified parking availability and required parking permits for all performers and volunteers.

■ The dress rehearsal was critical to the event's success, including theater logistics.

Recruiting Volunteer Reformers

When the dance choreographer and father first offered to dance to raise money for the center, I was thinking that I would also need to 'refresh' my Greek dancing steps and dust off my ballet shoes for a ballet solo. Instead, I reached out to our college community, our local church, children's center staff, and parents for performers. The response from volunteers was amazing; more than 75 individuals offered to help the center by performing for the two-hour fundraising event. Most of the volunteer performers were center parents and staff, college faculty, and the community — representing cultures as diverse as Greek, Latino, Hawaiian, English, Afghan, Indian, Korean, Chinese, Native American, Japanese, and American. In addition, one class of our day program preschoolers and teachers performed a song on stage — for the first time — holding their own handmade decorated microphones.

Cultivating In-kind Donations

While I was reading the performers' request forms (filled out with useful information including type of performance, duration, solo or group, costumes, lighting), I contacted the college's theater manager to ask about the cost and availability of the Big Theater, which can accommodate up to 1,200 people. Following a long and productive discussion, the manager offered the use of the Theater and his crew for free for the Children's Center fundraising performance. Having the Big Theater, the theater crew, and the 75 volunteer performers free of charge, was initially the biggest factor in our success. Wonderful attendance accounted for the rest.

Garnering Broad-based Involvement and Support

"Can't dance? Join our volunteer committee teams." Many center staff, parents, and college faculty volunteered their time, energy, and expertise by marketing and selling tickets, being ushers, and helping backstage during the dress rehearsal and on the night of the event.

Various departments from the college offered their expertise free of charge:

■ The college's graphic designer assisted in the creation of our logo, flyers, posters, tickets, programs, invitations for VIPs, thank-you notes, and certificates for the volunteer performers.

■ Media Services assisted with the printing of all marketing materials.

■ The college's media staff from the Art Department videotaped and photographed the event.

■ A student interviewed us and wrote an article before and after the event in the college's newspaper, *The Spectator*.

■ The college administration ran an article on our event in the monthly "Board of Trustees Report & Hotsheet."

■ A member of the college's foundation assisted in the box office in selling tickets.

■ Campus security provided us with complimentary parking permits for all volunteers.

■ The theater's stage crew provided us with very useful information on theater technical support and resources.

As long as we could provide a clear vision of what, why, and when we needed their help, college faculty and staff were willing to collaborate with us and join as a team for this good cause.

Finding Event Sponsors

We recognized that many of those involved in this fundraising event might hold a second job selling a product or a service or know someone who owns a small business. An email was sent to the college community, including center parents and staff promoting the opportunity to place a tax-deductible business advertisement in our event program. As a result of these efforts, our program was filled with many half-

and full-page advertisements marketing our community and its resources. Realtors, a catering business, dentists, cosmetic sales representatives, restaurant owners, parents wishing "good luck," and college departments supported our center by purchasing an ad in the event program.

Extending the Event

The event was a huge success! More than 500 people joined the audience and we surpassed our financial goal for the event. Planning an event that showcased diverse performers in a two-hour entertaining performance was a strategic marketing tool in and of itself. The event reached a wide audience coming from multicultural backgrounds, and each performance group brought to the theater its own circle of friends and family!

Today, a "Wall of Fame" stands in the center's lobby with the names of individuals who contributed to the success of this event, along with the article that appeared in the college newspaper. In addition, a documentation board displays quotes from the children on their favorite part of the performance, along with photographs of the event. A DVD of the event plays in the lobby, allowing everyone to revisit that magical evening, and the DVD has evolved into another item for fundraising. In addition, our local television channel airs the performance on a weekly basis, along with the center's contact information, attracting the audience's support and donations.

Using the Fundraiser to Build Collegiality within an ECD Program

Through this fundraising event, the relationship between the Children's Center staff and ECD faculty was strengthened:

■ The faculty advertised this event with their students.

■ Many faculty members gave extra credit to their students for attending the performance and completing an assignment relative to their course.

■ On the evening of the event, faculty members volunteered their time to sell and collect tickets and escort VIP attendees to their assigned seats.

Since the event, the center staff and ECD faculty have been brainstorming the possible use of funds towards the enhancement and beautification of the outdoor environment, a project that will directly benefit staff, children, lab students, and the ECD instructors.

Using a Fundraiser to Foster Community Partnerships

Besides raising funds for a worthwhile cause, this event helped to develop relationships between the Children's Center and the rest of the campus. It also helped foster community collaboration. New partnerships with other departments at the college were developed and existing relationships were strengthened. This fundraiser allowed the Children's Center to work for the first time as a part of a larger team. In addition, the fundraiser provided the opportunity for many volunteer performers and members of the audience to visit Chabot College for the first time, an excellent advertisement tool for increasing college students' enrollment and acquainting the community with the college's services and resources.

Building Future Fundraising Events

The magical night ended with a balloon and serpentine drop from the ceiling, as the performers were taking their final bow.

While celebrating the success of this fundraising event is important, investing time in writing thank-you notes of appreciation is equally important. Heartfelt thank-yous are a personal value of mine and a cultural responsibility. It is one way to cultivate partnerships, promote and keep the communication

lines open for future events. Many certificates of appreciation and thank-you notes were given to our volunteers and donors for their support and contribution. Parent volunteers, staff, and ECD faculty had a chance to experience a baklava treat as a gesture of appreciation and as a sweet memory until our next Children's Center fundraiser. When economic times are tough, receiving support from volunteers becomes even more valuable and meaningful.

Conclusion

In order to break the typical mold of annual fundraising ideas (e.g. t-shirts, flowerpots, and cookie sales), it took an unexpected downturn in financial resources to pique the Center community's passion and commitment to saving our evening program. Turning this situation into an opportunity for success depended in large part on the staff's innovativeness and effort. I continue to enjoy walking our college campus and being stopped by people who ask, "When is your next fundraising dance recital?"

Vicky Tsakoyias-Mendes

Vicky Tsakoyias-Mendes previously worked as a teacher and administrator at Bing Nursery School at Stanford University. She has been the Assistant Director of the Evening Program at Chabot College Children's Center for over seven years. Vicky holds bachelor's and master's degrees in Child Development and Business from educational institutions in Athens, Greece and in California. Her main research interests relate to directors' roles as leaders and advocates. She is a PITC graduate, and has served as a Director Mentor and as a member of Chabot College's Early Childhood adjunct faculty.

Securing and Managing Child Care Subsidies

by Judith Bordin

In 1994, the federal government passed the Personal Responsibility and Work Opportunity Reconciliation Act (PRWORA). It replaced Aid to Families and Dependent Children (AFDC) with Temporary Assistance to Needy Families (TANF) and heralded the emergence of welfare reform. One of the major issues that loomed large for the success of this program was child care. Welfare reform mandated that more parents enter the workforce and the need for care has increased.

The need for slots for these children became critical. Thus, many states have instituted *capacity building* programs. They encouraged licensed providers to enroll welfare-to-work families in their programs and receive a subsidy while the parents attend training or begin employment. This article reports the findings of a survey that asked providers about their motivation and experiences accepting subsidies in welfare reform.

What is subsidized child care under welfare reform?

Parents (with few exceptions) who are receiving welfare benefits must be employed in a job training program, or enrolled in an accredited school or college. If parents meet this requirement, they are eligible to receive a child care allowance. With this allowance, they may choose to enroll their child or children in a child care program. This care could be in center-based programs, family day care homes, or exempt care (where a family member or friend can receive payment for child care offered to one family).

A list of all licensed caregivers in one county was obtained from the local resource and referral agency. A total of 283 surveys were mailed, 57 (20.1%) were sent to child care centers, and 226 (79.8%) were sent to family day care providers. One hundred forty-four providers (50.5%) returned their surveys in the pre-addressed, stamped envelopes. Thirty-five child care centers (64.1 %) and 109 family day care providers (48.2%) responded to the survey. Eighty-two percent of the facilities had recent or current direct experience with the subsidy programs.

Why should programs participate in this program?

The most common provider response to this question in our survey was that subsidized care offered an opportunity to *fill a slot*. Many providers saw this program as an opportunity to provide enrollment for families who would need long-term child care.

Another response was a sincere desire on the part of caregivers to help these families. Many commented that, "it is great to be able to provide services to a cross section of our society," and that the subsidized families "need child care to move forward with their development." Others appreciated that the program allowed them to "be able to serve all families no matter what their needs" and "enable parents a chance to better themselves." Another had a larger view stating that subsidies "improve the whole economy."

How do providers learn of the programs in their area?

Providers indicated that they first became aware of the opportunities for participation in this program from other providers. This was accomplished at professional meetings, director support groups, or the *grocery store*. Secondly, many providers indicated newsletter articles from the local child care resource and referral agencies or other groups organized to plan for the child care community.

What are the procedures for becoming a subsidized program?

Most providers learned more detail about the subsidy programs through the child care resource and referral agency, the welfare office, or the local child care planning council. However, the subsidies are based upon parental choice. Thus, providers must make themselves known to parents who may have the subsidies. Resource and referral agencies will do this for providers by working closely with county welfare offices. In fact, many resource and referral agencies are mandated to provide swift information about child care to former welfare clients.

Many agencies have worked jointly to establish procedures for referrals and communicate with parents who need child care. Some welfare offices have *red phones* that are directly linked to the resource and referral agencies. Or, they may give postcards to parents to indicate their child care needs and mail them to the agency.

Some counties have established specific lists of providers for these families. In other words, parents would receive a list of providers who have current openings and are knowledgeable of program paperwork and policies. It is hoped that this approach will streamline enrollment for families and providers.

What are some of the problems that providers have encountered?

- **Timely Payments** — This issue was of greatest concern among providers. Larger, for-profit centers identified this as particularly important. They stated that their budgets were tight and late payments were a hardship. Additionally, some of the reimbursement rates in these programs were lower than non-subsidized family rates, making their reimbursement more critical.

- **Paperwork** — Providers were willing to complete the extra paperwork that was needed for these families, but lamented the confusing or ambiguous questions/statements that needed responses.

- **Parental Compliance with Program Requirements** — In some agencies, parents must submit all paperwork in order for the provider to be paid. This caused anxiety, concern, and a real problem for providers who must depend on parents to complete billing forms in order to receive payment.

- **Welfare Agency Inconsistency** — Providers felt confused by inconsistent responses to their questions from different agency workers. It seemed that the agency workers who administered the program were creating policies and procedures as the problems arose. It seemed that the answers to provider questions depended on who was on phone-day duty on that occasion.

■ **State Budget Delay** — Providers cited past experience with state budget delays that were very difficult for them. They worried that their participation in the program would make them vulnerable to overdue payments.

How can these problems be avoided?

Providers can carefully investigate the policies and procedures of the funding agency. Ask about the role of agency workers:

■ Is there a written manual?

■ What are the paperwork requirements?

■ What help can I expect from the welfare agency?

■ Are there other support agencies? If so, who are they and what is their role?

■ How are payments to child care providers authorized?

■ Do agency workers help in completing the forms?

■ Are they knowledgeable about the policies and procedures?

■ Do workers return phone calls promptly?

■ Are workers willing to visit the child care facility to talk with the provider or parents?

Why do providers stay enrolled in these programs?

Providers with experience serving these families were impressed with the changes that some of the families had made. They discussed the higher rates of organization in the households such as, 'children with cleaner clothes,' and 'an improvement in on time pick-up and delivery.' Providers also mentioned that families appreciated them and often asked household management or child-rearing questions. Providers

also thought that, overall, parents were proud of their accomplishments toward independence.

Where do I go for help with questions?

Provider associations and professional organizations may want to establish a working relationship with the agencies that administer these programs to address these issues. Providers can also join professionals from child care resource and referral agencies and planning councils to provide input into the process of child care subsidy programs.

It seems important for welfare-to-work agencies, child care providers, and others who assist them to work closely together to ensure the success of these programs for these families. If welfare reform is to flourish, child care providers must be included in a meaningful dialogue that encourages their active and enthusiastic participation.

Questions for child care providers to ask the welfare agency before participating in a subsidized program:

1. What services can I expect from the welfare office? the local resource and referral agency?

2. What paperwork needs to be submitted to receive payment?

3. How long does it take to get a check issued?

4. What kinds of paperwork are required each week, month, year? Who submits the paperwork for payment?

5. What role do parents play in this program? What do they have to do in order to comply with program policies?

6. Who do I call if I need help?

7. What is the best way to communicate with your agency?

8. Do you have a policy manual to govern this program? Are providers given a copy?

9. What happens if the legislature delays the approval of the state budget?

10. Does your agency meet regularly with child care organizations?

11. Do you anticipate any changes in your policies and procedures in the future? If so, what?

Judith Bordin

Judith Bordin is an associate professor of child development at California State University, Chico, teaching courses in staff relations, parenthood, and research methodology. In the past, she has consulted with Head Start, state preschools, and private child care organizations, and has nine years experience as the head teacher in a college laboratory school.

Ask and Ye Shall Receive

A Primer for Large-scale Fundraising

by Patricia Scallan Berl

In the past, large-scale fundraising activities went hand-in-hand with non-profit organizations. Today, in an increasingly competitive and challenging business environment, every center, whether large or small, non-profit or proprietary, single or multi-site, can benefit from a well-orchestrated fundraising campaign.

For child care directors, executing a successful fundraising plan can generate needed funds for daily operations or program expansions. Equally important, effective fundraising strengthens a center's image in the community and expands its market presence.

Fundraising will be a significant factor in maintaining the economic viability of many child care centers. Escalating costs of quality child care services necessitate supplementing income from parent tuitions and state and local subsidies.

Many centers are already turning to private individuals, corporations, and foundations that give over $10.5 billion annually to charitable causes. As the child care industry expands, competition for the funding sources will intensify. Directors must be prepared for the fundraising challenge ahead. Before you embark upon a fundraising campaign, consider the primary axiom of fundraising:

Successful fundraising lies in blending your organization's goals with the interests and needs of the community.

An effective fundraising plan takes into account six key elements. These are:

- **Gifts** — the amount of money you are seeking to raise

- **Prospects** — the people in your community who have both an interest in and a potential for contributing to your cause

- **Opportunity** — the benefit that is directly bestowed upon the donor as a result of giving

- **Appeal** — the urgency, immediacy, and inherent attraction of your proposal

- **Timing** — the time frame within which you seek contributions or make an appeal

- **Resources** — the financial and human potential you have available to commit to fundraising activities (this includes planning time and management time for board, paid staff, and volunteers)

Much has been written about the psychology of fundraising. Professionals carefully consider three basic questions: who to ask, when to ask, and how much to ask for. A simple analogy of cookie jar economics illustrates the basic elements of strategic fundraising.

Think back to when you were a child and desperately wanted a cookie. Unfortunately, at three years of age, you could not independently obtain the cookies (gift), which were safely tucked away in a container on the top cupboard shelf. To fulfill your need, you naturally sought any family members (prospects) who could deliver the cookies to you.

If you went to your father, who was absorbed in the Sunday afternoon football game, your request fell on deaf ears (poor opportunity). If you approached your older brother, you were apt to run into more disappointment since, out of sheer sibling rivalry, he would choose not to grant your request. If, however, you approached your mom (favorable prospect who could derive personal satisfaction, i.e., benefit from meeting your request, since she baked the cookies), you would likely meet with success providing that you met the following conditions:

■ You did not ask right before dinner (timing).

■ You were not greedy.

Naturally, your petition emphasized how much you needed those cookies to the one person who would feel the most fulfilled in having met your request (appeal). Having successfully obtained your cookies, you came again and again to that generous donor (resources) for additional cookies.

What's true in cookie economics is true in all organized fundraising programs: First, identify your organization's needs; second, translate these needs into financial goals; third, determine your prospects; fourth, approach potential donors being mindful of the timing and immediacy of your appeal; and fifth, package your request in ways that match the donor's needs, style, and level of giving.

There are many activities from which to choose when drafting a fundraising plan. In selecting the right activity, begin by determining your center's financial needs. Then, balance your fundraising goal against the financial and human resources you have available to commit to the task of raising money.

Effective fundraising takes planning and time, not only from the director, but also from paid staff and volunteers. Finally, whatever activity you choose, whether it is an annual fundraiser or a gala special event, be certain that it is consonant with the goals and values of your center and is acceptable to the community.

Below are several effective approaches for large-scale fundraising.

Annual fund drives. Annual fund drives are the bread and butter of professional fundraisers. These drives solicit donors annually by letter to contribute funds for the continued operation of the organization. Annual fund drives work because they capitalize on the fact that donors already believe in their cause and will support the organization. It is a fundraising fact that if people give once, they will usually give again. Annual fund drives are institutionalized and occur year after year, thereby expanding exponentially the number of donors and gifts that can be realized.

Capital campaigns are used to raise large amounts of money for capital improvements or program expansion. Capital campaigns selectively target donors who are capable of giving large contributions and have already demonstrated an interest in and willingness to donate to the organization. Capital campaigns are one-time events and focus 80% of available time on 10% of the potential donors who are most capable of giving 90% of the money needed.

Special events are particularly attractive to for-profit centers since they focus the community's attention on the organization and expand its community image.

Generally, special events such as house and garden tours, auctions, dinners, lecture series require an outlay of cash to produce the event and are time and labor intensive. Expenses to put on a special event can eat voraciously into the event's proceeds if not carefully monitored. Special events require a six- to eight-month lead time. Nevertheless, they can enhance an organization's image in the community and expand business presence.

Corporate philanthropy. Before you knock on corporate doors, remember that corporate giving is not just altruism. Corporations give because they realize tax benefits or see potential to expand their markets, e.g. McDonald's sponsorship of the Special Olympics. When making an appeal to corporate donors, consider how you will provide donor recognition. Before you can reasonably expect a corporation to make a contribution to your center, you must first demonstrate your organization's viability and the community needs, which you serve.

Finally, have clearly stated goals, long-range plans, experienced leadership, a competent staff, an involved and resourceful board, and a fiscally sound budget in place before corporate solicitation begins. Corporations expect their investments to pay off both in terms of donor recognition and community needs fulfilled.

Before outlining your center's fundraising strategy, define the organization's mission and programs, identify funding goals, allocate available financial and human resources, select an approach, plan well, start early, and think positively.

Ask and ye shall receive.

Patricia Scallan Berl

Patricia Scallan Berl is Division Vice President of the mid-Atlantic operations for Bright Horizons Family Solutions (www.brighthorizons.com) the world's leading provider of employer-sponsored child care, back-up care, early education, and work/life solutions, operating more than 600 child care and early education centers across the U.S., in Europe, and Canada. Patricia is a frequent contributor to *Exchange*. In addition to writing, she has a passion for Springer Spaniels and orchids.

People Giving to People

Executing an Annual Giving Campaign

by Patricia Scallan Berl

Increasingly, child care centers are seeking ways to expand financial resources beyond parent tuition. Toward this end, fundraising strategies are taking on a greater significance in enhancing the economic survival of non-profit centers.

While in the past fundraising was synonymous with flea markets, car washes, and door-to-door candy sales, today it requires a highly disciplined and managed process. Its success lies in:

■ a thorough understanding of the center's goals and objectives.

■ knowledge of the potential benefactors.

■ rigorous planning and follow up.

Most child care directors recognize the need for fundraising. Yet, they are reluctant to initiate fund development programs, lacking experience as well as understanding of well-established professional techniques for executing a successful campaign.

Gearing Up

Before you embark on a fundraising program, consider the first axiom of fundraising: people give to people. Since 1985, individuals have been contrib-

uting 90% of all private philanthropic dollars in the United States. Corporations and foundations give less than 10% of the total charitable giving. Clearly, the major source of philanthropy is the individual contributor. The fundraising challenge to directors is to tap the individual giver.

An effective fundraising campaign cannot be undertaken solely by the director. It must have the full understanding and support of the board of directors and the knowledgeable commitment of dedicated volunteers. The quality of this commitment among participants will define the scope of the fundraising campaign that can be realistically executed.

Annual Giving Campaigns

Fund drives, known as *annual giving campaigns*, are the most effective way to raise significant and supplemental operating funds for schools and centers. Because these campaigns directly target the current and potential families in your center, there is a strong incentive for donors to give. Furthermore, the inherent recurring nature of the annual giving campaign format reinforces the donor's connection with the center over time.

For the past seven years, I have conducted annual giving campaigns at two centers, raising an aggregate of over $150,000. In the course of conducting these campaigns, I have identified eight essential points for managing a successful fund drive. These are:

- Know why you are raising the money

- Set a financial goal

- Target the message

- Tailor the appeal

- Draft the letter

- Cultivate donor response

- Implement donor response

- Evaluate the campaign

Know Why You are Raising the Money

Before you initiate an annual giving campaign, stop and consider why you wish to raise the money. To answer this question, begin by defining what your center is: how it communicates its needs, goals, and objectives to the community. In fundraising circles, this exercise of introspection is a case statement. It includes the following: your statement of purpose, list of current goals and objectives, history, statement of current needs and future needs, financial resources, list of previous donors, and an analysis of the market. In preparing the case statement, define your center in concise terms that will help gain consensus among the board of directors.

Next, consider how your center fits into the broader community — its market. Unfortunately, the do-good mentality of most non-profits is not sufficient justification for donors to give to your cause. Successful fundraising depends upon fundamental marketing principles.

Barry Nicholson, consultant to the Funding Center in Washington, DC, sees it as the process of understanding and responding to the exchange relationship between the community and the non-profit organization. According to Nicholson:

"Centers usually emerge in response to perceived needs in the environment. But the environment is constantly changing; and, therefore, non-profits must remain sensitive to these changes or market requirements. Non-profits must recognize that they are something more than do-good entities, that they do not live in a vacuum. Market sensitivity requires that organizations continually look at their role in the community."

Summing up Nicholson, environments tend to dictate what people need, and this in turn dictates what organizations do. With an awareness of marketing principles, child care centers can examine their mission in light of the real (versus perceived) needs of the community.

Set a Financial Goal

Having identified your mission and needs, set a financial goal. Think realistically but think big, at least 50% more than you expect to raise. It is helpful to suggest a contribution amount sought from the donor. Left on their own, donors will frequently underestimate the amount of contribution needed. By specifying the size of the donation needed, chances are increased that the financial target will be attained.

Emphasizing 100% participation is also important, although personalized follow-ups are most effective when focused upon specific donors who have the greatest potential for giving significant contributions. In fundraising, as well as in business, the 80/20 Paretto rule applies — 80% of the funds you receive will come from 20% or fewer of the donors solicited.

Concrete objectives stated with clearly understood price tags — for example, "the addition of a $3,000 piece of climbing equipment to improve the play-scape for the two-year-olds" or "the creation of a continuing education fund for staff to pursue graduate education" — are appeals that attract donors. These goals have a visible and more lasting effect on your program and services.

Generally, avoid appeals aimed at improving administrative support. Computers in the office, while necessary, do not generate the same degree of interest as computers in the classroom.

Finally, determine the length of the campaign. Generally, six to eight weeks is a good rule of thumb since most responses will be received within 10 to 14 days of the appeal. Fund drives that extend beyond three months rarely justify the investment in time.

Target the Message

Identify potential donors and target the funding appeal to specific populations that share a mutuality of interest with your organization. Obviously, those who benefit most directly from your services — the families of the children in your center — are the primary donor base. But parents of current students are just one group within the universe of donors to whom you appeal.

Parents of former students who once benefited from your center, parents of children yet to come, and grandparents of presently enrolled students expand the potential donor base.

Secondarily, community service groups, vendors, and contractors who perform service for your center can also be considered as donor prospects. All have a stake in seeing that your center remains a viable and contributing organization in the community.

Tailor the Appeal

Tailoring a fundraising appeal can be one of the most challenging and creative aspects of the development process. It involves matching the donor's interests with the needs of your organization. Because people give to people and not to causes, the more you know about the donor's personal history, values, education, interests, and investment in your community, the greater your success at appealing to the mutuality of interests between your center and the prospective donors.

Each appeal should be designed around the profile and interests of the donor. Appeals to parents of current students can stress the urgency of receiving money now to enrich a specific program that directly benefits their children.

Appeals to parents of former students can remind the donor of the important start their child received from your school, and the value in supporting the center in its mission to others. Parents of younger sisters and brothers who will attend the center in the future can be approached from the perspective that future viability depends upon the availability of the resources now.

When approaching the grandparents of children in your center as prospective donors, two considerations should be given: 1) gain the parents' permission before soliciting grandparents for contributions, and 2) send some form of communication such as a newsletter or program brochure to the grandparents before mailing the appeal letter. Providing these guidelines are followed, grandparents can become a substantial donor group.

Finally, businesses, contractors, and all others who routinely provide services to the center can be approached from the perspective of the value your center adds to the community. When soliciting these groups, consider the length of time of the relationship, playing on the strength and continuity of that relationship.

Draft the Letter

The solicitation letter is the most direct way to reach donors. It consists of three parts: the letter; donor response card; and a return, school addressed, stamped envelope. Inserting a fact sheet, newsletter, or brochure of the school is also helpful to donors who are not currently parents in the center.

The length of the letter should be limited to a page and a half, single-spaced, with a large signature block. The addition of the names of your board of directors in reduced type in the upper left-hand margin contributes to a professional look.

In constructing the letter, do not exceed eight paragraphs. For the opening, identify your center, its goals, and student population. You also may include a few sentences of brief history about your center. In the following paragraph, define your needs and announce the fund drive. State the financial requirements needed to achieve your goals. Emphasize the urgency of the need, the necessity of the annual giving campaign, and budget constraints.

Next, restate the financial goal of the campaign, specify the amount of individual contribution needed, and stress everyone's participation. Explain the donor response card, time frame for making the response, and any follow up planned.

In the closing paragraphs, reaffirm your need and reiterate the importance of the campaign's success. Express gratitude for the donor's consideration and participation.

Cultivate Donors

Many annual giving campaigns include a pre-appeal telephone contact with targeted donors to introduce the program and to entice special interest. Other campaigns send out solicitation letters, then follow up with a call to answer questions about the campaign, thereby encouraging each donor's careful consideration of appropriate levels of giving.

Social events such as receptions, dinners, and home-school events can provide a forum for introducing the annual campaign. Peer solicitation from parents to parents is most effective, as their common interests are integrated with the challenges and benefits of the campaign drive.

Implement Donor Response

The donor response card will help you track your donor and follow up pledge contributions. It will also provide you with the information necessary to update your mailing lists for subsequent fund drives. The response card includes donor name, status (parent of current child enrolled at the center, grandparent, friend of organization, board member), address, and contribution amount or pledge amount with date specified when pledge will be made. This card accompanies the donor's contribution, serves as the record, and becomes the future base for next year's donor list.

Respond to donors with a pre-written thank-you note that contains a blank for filling in the contribution amount. Add a written word of thanks at the end and personally sign all acknowledgments. A copied letter is useful. The original copy is sent to the parent and the copy is your record.

Evaluate the Campaign

Be sure to correct your donor lists against information provided from the return donor response card. Analyze your campaign results and establish next year's goals on the basis of your experience. If donors give once, they will give again, so continually follow up.

Remember, people give to people: believe in your organization and, above all, believe in yourself. Ask confidently for what you want, do not settle for less, and begin now!

Carefully executed, your annual fund campaign effort will not only generate ongoing financial support but will, additionally, and of equal importance, enhance your center's presence in the community.

Patricia Scallan Berl

Patricia Scallan Berl is Division Vice President of the mid-Atlantic operations for Bright Horizons Family Solutions (www.brighthorizons.com) the world's leading provider of employer-sponsored child care, back-up care, early education, and work/life solutions, operating more than 600 child care and early education centers across the U.S., in Europe, and Canada. Patricia is a frequent contributor to Exchange. In addition to writing, she has a passion for Springer Spaniels and orchids.

Shared Services

A Powerful Strategy to Support Sustainability of ECE Businesses

by Louise Stoney

As co-Founder of the Alliance for Early Childhood Finance, it's my job to think about how we pay for early care and education (ECE) services in the United States. I am actually pretty good at identifying creative, new financing strategies. But I can't make it simple. Generating the operating revenue needed to establish and sustain a high-quality ECE program has never been easy — and in a recession economy it is becoming even more difficult. To be sustainable, ECE managers must tap and blend many funding streams, deal with multiple public and private agencies, and effectively market their services to families. To keep these dollars flowing they must not only comply with a dizzying array of funding requirements, but also ensure that their program meets an increasingly complex set of quality standards. Add in all of the daily demands — staff that need supervision, a child who needs developmental screening or special health care or just won't stop biting, an anxious new parent, a clogged toilet, an ill cook — and who has the time or energy to deal with high finance? In short, running a successful ECE business can be a herculean job. I have profound respect for directors who are able to effectively juggle these competing demands, but I also worry that our field is losing leaders who are deeply skilled in child development simply because they are tired of struggling with the business side of the equation.

These worries led me to a new quest. If I couldn't make ECE finance simple, was there a way to help ECE businesses more easily manage the complexity? Was there a way to approach finance that not only generated additional dollars, but also helped ECE businesses succeed? I went in search of mentors and one of my first stops was Phil Acord, Executive Director of the Children's Home in Chattanooga, Tennessee. The Children's Home directly operates a child development center for 300 children, six weeks through five years of age, and also provides management services to ten additional community-based early childhood programs that collectively serve over 370 additional children. Programs affiliated with the Children's Home not only provide high-quality early care and education, but are also able to offer regular child assessment and classroom supports, as well as comprehensive services to children and their families with low incomes. Participating programs range in size; some are as small as 12 children and the largest serves 75.

Phil Acord is an impressive man. Many would call him herculean. But as I talked with him, and looked closely at the Children's Home structure, I soon realized that the model worked because Phil's leadership was backed by a strong network of staff. Just like the man in the Verizon commercial who is able to confront his adversary because he's got a network behind him, the business model and staffing structure created by Children's Home is what makes it strong. And as I continued my quest, seeking other mentors and other models, I saw a pattern. Some high-quality ECE programs have learned how to reach an economy of scale and still maintain the small, intimate settings that families prefer by using a strategy I have come to call shared services.

What is Shared Services?

The notion of shared services is pretty simple: it is a structure that enables organizations with common needs to share costs. Every day, when you slip your debit card into a gas pump or an ATM machine, you are using a shared service. Financial institutions have developed — and jointly finance — a very complex technology network that allows dollars to move easily among institutions. This shared infrastructure, built on common industry standards, makes it possible for banks to operate quickly and efficiently. State ECE leaders have begun to craft industry-wide standards (such as professional development systems and quality rating systems), but the ECE industry has yet to create the infrastructure and supports individual programs and providers need to not only comply with these standards but to operate efficiently. Phil Acord is part of a small but growing movement focused on changing that reality. A handful of early care and education leaders are crafting and testing business models, or shared platforms, that enable center- and home-based ECE programs to offer high-quality services and also succeed as small businesses.

Quite frequently, after hearing a presentation on shared services, someone will remark that shared services is not a new idea at all; that it sounds a lot like family child care networks and ECE industry chains. In many ways the idea is not new. What is unique about shared services, however, is the relationship to power. Traditionally, family child care networks were formed to monitor home-based sites and ensure that they met quality standards. And child care chains (proprietary and non-profit) are typically owned by

or accountable to corporate headquarters. These are what I would call 'power over' management strategies. Shared service alliances, on the other had, are a 'power with' management strategy.

The entities that participate in a shared service alliance not only agree to share policies and staff and an accountability structure; they have a stake in decision-making and benefit from the results. For example, family child care providers that become part of Infant Toddler Family Day Care (a home-based alliance in Fairfax, Virginia) join a legal trust (structured as a limited liability corporation), which contracts with a third party (IFDC) to manage fiscal, administrative, and professional development tasks. The home-based businesses that join the IFDC trust vote each year on how much of their fees will be spent to support administration and also help inform a range of decisions made by IFDC staff.

Participating providers are willing to pay a portion of their revenues to IFDC because what they receive in return is well worth it; they don't have to market their services (IFDC recruits families), or manage money (IFDC sends them a check twice a month), or find and pay for the required training; and they aren't isolated. Similarly, child care centers that join Sound Child Care Solutions (an alliance in Seattle, Washington) are asked to assess the strengths and interests of their staff prior to joining the alliance. The management at SCCS — both in the central office as well as in the centers — works as a team; a staff person who is skilled at human resources might take on that function for all centers in the alliance, while one who is good at curriculum development and support might assume that alliance-wide role. In some cases, alliances begin with a strong intermediary that reaches out to a group of providers, offering to develop a shared management structure.

In other cases, the alliance grows out of a desire to share resources. In the seacoast region of New Hampshire, for instance, a group of child care center directors met over lunch for one year to talk about how they could share costs. The result is a new,

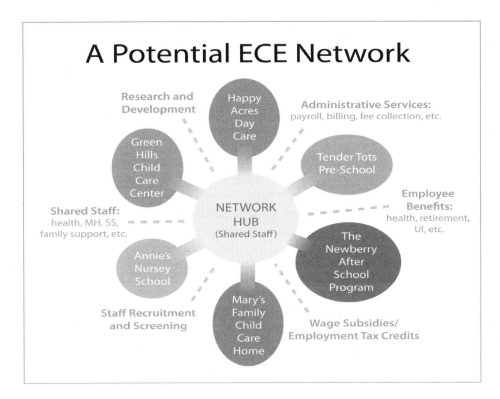

A Potential ECE Network

Research and Development

Happy Acres Day Care

Administrative Services: payroll, billing, fee collection, etc.

Green Hills Child Care Center

Tender Tots Pre-School

NETWORK HUB (Shared Staff)

Employee Benefits: health, retirement, UI, etc.

Shared Staff: health, MH, SS, family support, etc.

Annie's Nursey School

The Newberry After School Program

Staff Recruitment and Screening

Mary's Family Child Care Home

Wage Subsidies/ Employment Tax Credits

shared service alliance, led by Early Learning New Hampshire, which will begin in fall 2009.

Shared service business models can take many forms. In Chattanooga, Tennessee, the entity that leads the effort and employs shared staff is a large child development center, the Children's Home. Before offering management services to the ten community-based programs in the network, Phil Acord already employed staff to manage money and support program quality. Creating the network involved restructuring and expanding that staff to reach an additional 370 off-site children. In short, there was a natural economy of scale that made a shared services approach affordable and possible.

In other communities similar economies of scale can be found in a range of intermediary organizations within — and outside of — early care and education, including Child Care Resource and Referral (CCR&R) agencies, family child care networks, nonprofit umbrella organizations, and others. Or participating ECE programs may decide to join forces and create their own, collectively run, shared services entity.

Many options are possible, including the following:

Program Alliance — Independent ECE businesses contract with a common administrative agency to handle some or all aspects of program administration and fiscal management

Consortium — Existing ECE businesses join together as a single non-profit entity Provider Trust — ECE providers form and join a legal trust (structured as a limited liability corporation), which contracts with a third party to manage fiscal and administrative tasks

Cooperative — ECE providers create a jointly owned entity that assumes responsibility for administration in multiple, independent sites

Growing Support from Funders

Private foundations, business leaders, and policy makers are intrigued by the possibility of shared platforms for the early care and education industry:

- The Annie E. Casey Foundation is helping their Atlanta and Baltimore civic sites explore shared services.

- The David and Laura Merage Foundation is leading a statewide shared services effort in Colorado.

- The William Penn Foundation is engaged in a Philadelphia feasibility study.

- The Mimi and Peter Haas Fund is looking at the strategy to support and strengthen their Model Centers.

- United Way has been a leader, or a key support, for local alliances in Colorado, Iowa, New Hampshire, Ohio, Tennessee, Washington, and other communities.

- A new alliance in Rockland County, New York, received funds from a state innovations grant program supported by federal Child Care and Development Block Grant (CCDF) funds.

- A Colorado alliance has received a grant funded by the Temporary Assistance for Needy Families (TANF) dollars.

- The New Hampshire alliance is tapping community development funds for start-up.

Funders recognize that a shared service approach offers benefits for children, families, and the ECE industry as a whole, including:

■ professional fiscal management and economic strength of a larger organization makes it easier for very small businesses to weather economic ebbs and flows.

■ more career opportunities and better working conditions, wages, and benefits for staff.

■ lower costs from economies of scale in business functions like payroll, benefits management, banking, janitorial, food services, and purchasing.

■ higher-quality early childhood education, and the ability to offer a range of comprehensive family support services, due to a more stable financial and organizational structure and a comprehensive approach to professional development.

■ better data and school transitions, via centralized systems, assessments, and technology to support outcomes-tracking, reflective practice, and linkages with school districts.

In these tough economic times many industries are struggling to survive. Even leading U.S. industries — automakers, energy companies, banks — are learning they must challenge their old business models and reinvent themselves. Many of these industries are engaging in collaborative ventures and shared platforms. Early care and education businesses are no exception. Our industry has been doing the same thing, in essentially the same way, for many years. It's time to join this movement for change; to open our minds, look beyond traditional concepts of competition, and begin to test out new, shared business strategies.

For more information on shared services for the ECE industry, check out the Shared Services Toolkit and other resources at www.earlylearningventures.org

---

There are many ways to administer shared services. The 'hub' agency can be a large early care and education provider, a Resource and Referral agency, a family child care network, or another intermediary organization within — or outside of — the ECE field. Background information on a range of options is available in the Shared Services Toolkit: http://merage.org/index. asp?w=pages&r=85&pid=115

Louise Stoney

Louise Stoney is an independent consultant specializing in early care and education (ECE) finance and policy, and Co-Founder of both Opportunities Exchange and the Alliance for Early Childhood Finance. Louise has worked with state and local governments, foundations, ECE providers, industry intermediaries, research and advocacy groups in over 40 states. Public and private organizations have sought Louise's expertise to help craft new finance and policy options, as well as write issue briefs on challenging topics. She has helped model ECE program costs, revise subsidy policy and rate-setting strategies, re-visit QRIS standards and procedures, craft new approaches to contracting and voucher management, and more. Louise holds a Master's Degree in Social Work from the State University of New York at Stony Brook.

Details on the Children's Home Shared Service Alliance

The Children's Home, a non-profit agency, directly operates a child development center and also provides management services to ten community-based early childhood programs. Five of the community-based sites are independent non-profit child care centers. The remaining five sites are located in public schools. Only one of the community-based sites has a full-time, on-site director. Management in the remaining sites is provided by staff, hired by the Children's Home who work as a team and divide their time among the sites. Each program has a manager on site at least half-time. One (or more) lead teachers at each site is the designated 'go to' person in the event that management staff is not on site. Off-site centers also share staff in the Finance, Maintenance, and Food Service departments.

Each of the five independent sites has its own board of directors, which negotiates a management contract with the Children's Home. The Treasurer and Board for each site work with the Children's Home CEO in developing the annual budget, and must approve it each year. All fiscal and administrative services are coordinated, using the same automated systems and reports. Children's Home staff process payroll and administer benefits for all sites. The Children's Home collectively negotiates contracts to cover the following services at all sites: liability, health, and disability insurance; maintenance and janitorial services, supplies and equipment; and food purchasing. Frequently, donations are distributed to the entire network.

All sites use the Creative Curriculum™ and all are required to participate in the Tennessee Star Quality Rating System. STARS's monitors conduct annual classroom assessments at each site. The Children's Home staff ensures, however, that each site is prepared to succeed and therefore conducts informal observations and assessments when necessary. Teacher in-service training is frequently conducted with staff from all ten sites.

For more information on the Children's Home shared service alliance, including an organizational chart, job descriptions, sample contract, and a video of the program, go to: http://merage.org/index.asp?w=pages&r=85&pid=115.